3995

CYBERSAFETY

Living with the Internet

CYBERSAFETY

CYBERSAFETY

Living with the Internet

SAMUEL C. MCQUADE, III, PH.D.
and
SARAH E. GENTRY

CONSULTING EDITOR

MARCUS K. ROGERS, Ph.D., CISSP, DFCP
Founder and Director,
Cyber Forensics Program,
Purdue University

CHELSEA HOUSE
An Infobase Learning Company

Cybersafety: Living with the Internet

Chelsea House
An Infobase Learning Company
132 West 31st Street
New York NY 10001

Library of Congress Cataloging-in-Publication Data
McQuade, Samuel C.
  Living with the Internet / Samuel C. McQuade, III and Sarah Gentry.
    p. cm. — (Cybersafety)
  Includes bibliographical references and index.
  ISBN-13: 978-1-60413-697-5 (hardcover : alk. paper)
  ISBN-10: 1-60413-697-9 (hardcover : alk. paper) 1. Internet—Social aspects. 2. Online social networks. 3. Internet—Safety measures. I. Gentry, Sarah. II. Title. III. Series.
  HM851.M397 2011
  303.48'33—dc22   2011005646

Chelsea House books are available at special discounts when purchased in bulk quantities for businesses, associations, institutions, or sales promotions. Please call our Special Sales Department in New York at (212) 967-8800 or (800) 322-8755.

You can find Chelsea House on the World Wide Web at http://www.infobasepublishing.com

Text design by Erik Lindstrom
Cover design by Takeshi Takahashi
Composition by EJB Publishing Services
Cover printed by Yurchak Printing, Landisville, Pa.
Book printed and bound by Yurchak Printing, Landisville, Pa.
Date printed: March 2012

Printed in the United States of America

This book is printed on acid-free paper.

All links and Web addresses were checked and verified to be correct at the time of publication. Because of the dynamic nature of the Web, some addresses and links may have changed since publication and may no longer be valid.

CONTENTS

Foreword

The Internet has had and will continue to have a profound effect on society. It is hard to imagine life without such technologies as computers, cell phones, gaming devices, and so on. The Internet, World Wide Web, and their associated technologies have altered our social and personal experience of the world. In no other time in history have we had such access to knowledge and raw information. One can search the Library of Congress, the Louvre in Paris, and read online books and articles or watch videos from just about any country in the world. We can interact and chat with friends down the street, in another state, or halfway around the globe. The world is now our neighborhood. We are a "wired" society that lives a significant amount of our life online and tethered to technology.

The Internet, or cyberspace, is a great enabler. What is also becoming apparent, though, is that there is a dark side to this global wired society. As the concept of who our friends are moves from real world relationships to cyberspace connections, so also do the rules change regarding social conventions and norms. How many friends do we have online that we have actually met in person? Are online-only friends even real or at the very least whom they claim to be? We also begin to redefine privacy. Questions arise over what should be considered private or public information. Do we really want everyone in the global society to have access to our personal information? As with the real world there may be people online that we do not wish to associate with or grant access to our lives.

It is easy to become enamored with technology and the technology/information revolution. It is equally as easy to become paranoid about the dangers inherent in cyberspace. What is difficult but necessary is to be realistic about how our world has been forever changed. We see numerous magazine, TV, and newspaper headlines regarding the latest cybercrime attacks. Stories about identity theft being the fastest growing nonviolent criminal activity are common. The government is concerned with cyber or information warfare attacks against critical infrastructures. Given this kind of media coverage it is easy to think that the sky is falling and cyberspace is somehow evil. Yet if we step back and think about it, technology is neither good nor bad, it simply *is*. Technology is neutral; it is what we do with technology that determines whether it improves our lives or damages and makes our lives more difficult. Even if someone is on the proverbial fence over whether the Internet and cyberspace are society enablers or disablers, what is certain is that the technology genie is out of the bottle. We will never be able to put it back in; we need to learn how to master and live with it.

Learning to live with the Internet and its technological offshoots is one of the objectives behind the Cybersafety series of books. The immortal words of Sir Francis Bacon (the father of the scientific method), "knowledge is power," ring especially true today. If we live in a society that is dependent on technology and therefore we live a significant portion of our daily lives in cyberspace, then we need to understand the potential downside as well as the upside. However, what is not useful is fear mongering or the demonization of technology.

There is no doubt that cyberspace has its share of bad actors and criminals. This should not come as a surprise to anyone. Cyberspace mirrors traditional society, including both the good and unfortunately the bad. Historically criminals have been attracted to new technologies in an effort to improve and extend their criminal methods. The same advantages that technology and cyberspace bring to our normal everyday lives (e.g., increased communication, the ability to remotely access information) can be used in a criminal manner. Online fraud, identity theft, cyberstalking, and cyberbullying are but a few of the ugly behaviors that we see online today.

Navigating successfully through cyberspace also means that we need to understand how the "cyber" affects our personality and social behavior. One of the empowering facets of cyberspace and technology is the fact that we can escape reality and find creative outlets for ourselves. We can immerse ourselves in computer and online games, and if so inclined, satisfy our desire to gamble or engage in other risky behaviors. The sense of anonymity and the ability to redefine who we are online can be intoxicating to some people. We can experiment with new roles and behaviors that may be polar opposites of who we are in the real physical world. Yet, as in the real world, our activities and behaviors in cyberspace have consequences too. Well-meaning escapism can turn to online addictions; seemingly harmless distractions like online gaming can consume so much of our time that our real world relationships and lives are negatively affected. The presumed anonymity afforded by cyberspace can lead to bullying and stalking, behaviors that can have a profound and damaging impact on the victims and on ourselves.

The philosophy behind the Cybersafety series is based on the recognition that cyberspace and technology will continue to play an increasingly important part of our everyday lives. The way in which we define who we are, our home life, school, social relationships, and work life will all be influenced and impacted by our online behaviors and misbehaviors. Our historical notions of privacy will also be redefined in terms of universal access to our everyday activities and posted musings. The Cybersafety series was created to assist us in understanding and making sense of the online world. The intended audience for the series is those individuals who are and will be the most directly affected by cyberspace and its technologies, namely young people (i.e., those in grades 6–12).

Young people are the future of our society. It is they who will go forward and shape societal norms, customs, public policy, draft new laws, and be our leaders. They will be tasked with developing positive coping mechanisms for both the physical and cyberworlds. They will have dual citizenship responsibilities: citizens of the physical and of the cyber. It is hoped that this series will assist in providing insight, guidance, and positive advice for this journey.

The series is divided into books that logically gather related concepts and issues. The goal of each book in the series is not to scare but to educate and inform the reader. As the title of the series states the focus is on "safety." Each book in the series provides advice on what to watch out for and how to be safer. The emphasis is on education and awareness while providing a frank discussion related to the consequences of certain online behaviors.

It is my sincere pleasure and honor to be associated with this series. As a former law enforcement officer and current educator, I am all too aware of the dangers that can befall our young people. I am also keenly aware that young people are more astute than some adults commonly give them credit for being. Therefore it is imperative that we begin a dialogue that enhances our awareness and encourages and challenges the reader to reexamine their behaviors and attitudes toward cyberspace and technology. We fear what we do not understand; fear is not productive, but knowledge is empowering. So let's begin our collective journey into arming ourselves with more knowledge.

—Marcus K. Rogers, Ph.D., CISSP, DFCP,
Founder and Director,
Cyber Forensics Program,
Purdue University

Introduction

According to a recent series of Pew Internet & American Life Project reports, 75 percent of American teenagers 12 to 17 years of age own a cell phone, 93 percent of teens and young adults ages 18 to 29 go online, and three out of four adults of all ages periodically connect to the Internet.[1] Of American adults who use the Internet, 60 percent use high-speed broadband connections from home and 55 percent connect wirelessly, whether at home or on the go using devices like cell/smart phones or laptop computers.[2] "Some 19 percent of Internet users now say they use Twitter or another service to share updates about themselves, or to see updates about others."[3] In 2009, 65 percent of teens and 48 percent of adults used a social networking site like MySpace, Facebook or LinkedIn.[4] These and many more statistics reveal that Americans are getting online and becoming more connected than ever before. Indeed, people throughout the world are living with the Internet in all sorts of ways.

HOW ANNA AND HER FAMILY
LIVE WITH THE INTERNET

Anna Snowden lives with her parents in a suburb located in New York State. She is 13 years old, in eighth grade, and an average student who plays flute and participates in cheerleading. Her 21-year-old brother no longer lives at home. Everyone in her family uses the Internet every day at home, at school, and at work to manage the family-owned business. Anna likes to use computers and her cell phone, especially while hanging out with her friends. For instance, immediately after getting ready for school, Anna uses her mom's old laptop computer to jump onto Facebook to check her account. Before leaving her house she is looking for messages from people she has "friended" online. New items include responses to messages she posted the previous day, as well as comments on photos, status updates, and new friend requests that she has accepted. Anna comments back and forth rapidly using abbreviations whenever possible in order to speed up her *instant messaging* and earn respect among her friends who are doing the same thing.

Anna's weekly school schedule consists of several classes, a study hall session, and lunchtime. This year she is studying earth science, global history, English, algebra, Spanish, art, child development, and photography. She works hard in her classes and takes pride in her school accomplishments. Anna uses a school computer and the Internet in most of her classes, especially in photography, which includes tutorials for using Photoshop software. When finished early with an in-class photography assignment, Anna and other students, who figured out how to unlock Facebook in school, can access the social network using a school computer when the teacher is not looking. For Anna, this is a sneaky treat because her cell phone allows only for texting and making calls. She is envious of other kids who have more expensive devices like the iPhone, BlackBerry, or iPod Touch that enable them to use the Net at any time. Her school allows students to use their personal devices during lunch, study hall, between classes, and occasionally in class if teachers say it is okay, but a lot of kids find ways to sneak online throughout the school day when they are not supposed to. Anna says that after school and well into the evening hours, she normally goes back online using her mom's old laptop to do homework and to post comments to the Web pages of some 600 online "friends," only a portion of whom she actually knows in person.

Before he graduated from high school, Anna's older brother engaged in online gaming and used Facebook a lot. These days, however, since he began working full time, he doesn't have time to *socially compute* as much as he once did, though he still enjoys video games on the weekends. Anna's mother and father also use computers and the Internet for many things related to their sign-painting business and for personal things like e-mailing friends and shopping online. Their online business activities include receiving customer orders; researching company logos, trademarks, and sign dimensions; designing new signs; processing account records; ordering supplies; and paying bills online.

Everyone in Anna's family uses the Internet differently according to their needs and interests. As for Anna, at the end of another fast-paced day that included combinations of online and off-line activities, she goes to bed but not before checking her cell phone one last time for incoming text messages in a digital chain of never-ending chat.

The Internet plays a vital role in everyday lives of most people, and certainly for everyone who lives in modern computerized societies. Nearly 2 *billion* people—about one in four people on the planet—now regularly use computers, cell phones, personal digital assistants (PDAs), or other types of electronic information technology (IT) devices. When using IT, people often, although not always, access the Internet to connect to an entire world of other online users. People who now regularly use the Internet include young and older persons, students and working professionals, and everyone else whose mind is engaged while online. In general, users can access the Internet at any time and from anywhere wired or wireless connections are available. Once online they can engage in an infinite assortment of activities. Connecting to the Net now occurs from

New technological gadgets allow people to connect to the Internet in faster and more convenient ways. Students who use the Internet for schoolwork can access information on their laptop, iPad, or smart phone. *(Source: AP Photo/Las Cruces Sun-News)*

homes, schools, workplaces, and while people are on the go, as with mobile computing. And the fundamental reason people connect to the Internet is to communicate with each other.

Today, thousands of IT manufacturers and Internet service provider (ISP) companies provide computer-related products and services to IT users throughout the world. Although computer and telecom products can be expensive to purchase and operate, IT is increasingly affordable for businesses and individual consumers. Hardware such as computers, media players, scanners, gaming devices, and cell phones make it possible for people to communicate, do research, learn, go shopping, manage their finances, and enjoy music, movies, and games online from almost anywhere.

Hardware and very fast broadband Internet connections are actually complex computer and telecommunications systems powered by electricity. Information systems typically consist of wired and wireless components through which an electrical current operates the digital switching and signaling (on-off) operating systems of computing devices. Software applications installed on hardware devices (such as computers, cell phones, and PDAs) enable millions of people throughout the world to communicate, be productive, and enjoy themselves.

Computerization occurs when a majority of people in a society come to rely on IT for basic, everyday needs. Computerization develops over many years of technological progress and social change, and it is not necessary for everyone in a society to use computers, other types of IT devices, or the Internet for the process to occur. Today the Internet is used for sending and receiving data in support of: military national defense, manufacturing, transportation, agriculture and food production, financial services, health care, education, engineering, research, technology development, entertainment, and many other purposes. Chances are that anyone living in a computerized country like the United States, Canada, or the United Kingdom already uses a computer and a cell phone or a similar IT device to connect to the Internet. Other computerized countries include France, Germany, Sweden, Switzerland, Israel, India, Japan, South Korea, China, Malaysia, and Australia. People living in these nations or in other regions of the world, including in the Middle East, South America, and Africa, are also increasingly online and relying on computers, cell phones, and the Internet for many things in their lives.

This book is about how people live with the Internet and how they use *the Net* and rely on it for their routine and emergency communications and for many other things related to exchanging information. The first thing explained is what the Internet is, how it came to be used, how it works, and how big it is as it continues to expand throughout the world. A brief history of technological inventions describes how early calculating devices lead to computers and eventually the Internet. The history alludes to many social and cultural developments surrounding technological inventions and innovations that established conditions for how people today live with the Internet. Next, it is explained in more detail how the Internet is used mostly for good purposes through various professional and personal interactions. In the process this book will look at how Facebook and many other Web-enabled forums and social networks are increasingly being used for educational, professional, and social interactions; how the Internet is enabling technologies and therefore human beings to interconnect seamlessly; and that the future is filled with hopes and concerns about the power and potential intrusions that computing may have in people's lives.

For all its obvious and potential benefits, the Internet also presents risks to all people who use it. These risks include many forms of harmful and even criminal activities such as computer hacking, password cracking, creating and distributing harmful computer code, cyberbullying, cyberstalking, financial fraud, digital piracy, academic dishonesty, and many other types of online misbehavior. All Internet users must understand these risks if they are to be safe and secure when using the Internet.

What Is the Internet?

Dan is 28 years old. He works at a technology firm and enjoys console and online gaming. He plays a variety of games on his Nintendo Wii. His high-tech Wii connects to the Internet wirelessly through his home network. When Dan's friends visit, they use the Internet channel on Wii, which is actually a Web browser built into the console gaming device. This allows them to access Web sites such as YouTube, Facebook, and many other sites used for entertainment. Millions of people enjoy using the Internet in similar ways while at home, at school, at work, and while on the go.

Dan grew up using computers. He understands that the Internet is a vast information system, powered by a massive computer network consisting of innumerable smaller computer networks that enable millions of people to connect with each other simultaneously while using computers, cell phones, or other types of IT devices.

In college Dan studied information technology and software engineering. He is not an expert, but he knows there is only one Internet. And because the word Internet is the proper name of the world's largest computer network, it should be capitalized when spelled in English. However, the Internet is often referred to simply as "the Net" or "the Web," the latter of which is an abbreviation for the World Wide Web (WWW). Technically speaking however, the WWW is not the same thing as the Internet. Rather, the Web consists of information, or content, that rests on the information infrastructure technology of the Internet. Information infrastructure includes millions of computers interconnected with wired and/or wireless telecommunications (phone) systems. Knowing the difference between the Internet and WWW is especially important to computer scientists and engineers who work in technical fields that involve hardware and software technology design and interactions.

When using the Internet at work, Dan considers how computers, cell phones, PDAs, and gaming devices can be used to help enrich the lives of people in ways that are productive, enjoyable, legal, and which do not cause harm to other people encountered online (virtually) or in person (face to face). This is very challenging because people use the Internet for many different things. They also live in, and sometimes work or study in, many different countries, all having unique cultures. Different cultures throughout the world maintain different values, beliefs, customs, laws, and monetary systems, as well as different ways for acceptably using technology. Thus, Dan, as a thoughtful IT professional and responsible user of the Net, thinks through how people interacting online can and should use the Internet responsibly so that as many people as possible can be productive and enjoy their lives when using the Internet.

The Internet as it is now commonly thought about and used has existed only since 1993, when WWW content became searchable by using browser software. However, the concept and practice of social networking without computers existed in ancient civilizations. Prior to the discovery of electricity, communications between people were limited to oral conversations in various languages and later also written messages created with pens, pencils, and paper. Eventually basic methods of communicating would be revolutionized by telegraph, telephone, and computer systems.

A BRIEF HISTORY OF INFORMATION TECHNOLOGIES (IT)

Early peoples sometimes sent and received messages via trusted couriers who carried confidential or secret encoded messages in sealed pouches. Messages could be sent and received over distances on land or sea using different colored and shaped objects or flags called semaphores. This practice, known as optical telegraphy, was often accomplished with the aid of a telescope that allowed people to see signals made with flags, signs, or positioning of objects from far away. Semaphore stations were located on hilltops long distances apart. They consisted of a small living area and tall tower on which adjustable arms could be rotated in various ways to represent letters and spell out words. After a message was received, it could be confirmed and then forwarded to people manning one or more other semaphore stations located in a chain across a landscape. In this way, important messages could be sent quickly over long distances as when needed to convey changing circumstances affecting armies on land or navy ships at sea. Semaphores were also used to send messages from city to city to communicate important government announcements or market prices for crops. Though very important in its time, semaphore technology was cumbersome to use and often resulted in the meaning of messages becoming confused.

As more people in early societies learned to read and write, typesetting machines and the printing press expanded and improved upon the quality of messaging technology. By 1450 A.D., printing technology made it possible to quickly produce many copies of documents such as books, newspapers, purchasing catalogs, and magazines. These and other forms of printed documents forever changed the nature of social networking. Mass communications like newspapers that reported daily events, along with merchandise catalogs and books written about many subjects, all inspired new thinking and sharing of ideas among people.

This signalman is waving a semaphore message to other ships in an Allied convoy traveling across the Atlantic Ocean in 1943. Semaphore signaling with flags or visual cues was a popular way of communicating over long distances. *(Source: AP Photo)*

Though very important, printing messages in bulk did not by itself help messages to be distributed to specific locations or among particular people who needed to communicate with each other. Eventually printing technology was combined with postal mail and express freight services to send and receive messages and packages from one address to another. For a relatively low cost, a lightweight, sealed (and therefore privately intended) message could be routed from one person or location to another either via stagecoach, railroad, and/or steamship. The Pony Express, a horseback mail delivery service famous throughout the American West in the early 1860s, was often combined with other ways to send messages, such as by telegraph or stagecoach. Together these were relied on for relatively fast delivery of letters and very small packages. Eventually various forms of transportation, combined with a large system of post offices, freight stations, and drop-off mail boxes, allowed people living in big cities or rural areas to receive messages and packages of all sizes in a timely and reliable manner. With these innovations people became more connected to each other and to what was happening in the world.

Throughout history people have struggled to invent faster, more reliable, and less expensive ways to send and receive messages and packages. This is as true for people living today as it was for people living hundreds of years ago. People living today still use most forms of communication that were used in earlier times, along with computers, phones, and the Internet. People use Express Mail and freight services in ways used a century ago (e.g., via truck or train), but they can now also use jets and the Internet to send and even track messages or packages they have already sent.

While they were trying to improve upon the delivery of their messages, people have also sought to conceal and protect messages from being detected, intercepted, and read or interpreted as in secret government communications or very private correspondence between individuals. Indeed, living with the Internet and digital communications enabled by modern IT involves all of these same challenges: affordability, timeliness, reliability, privacy, security, and safety for everyone involved.

Mass Electronic Communications: Telegraph, Telephone, Radio, and Television Technologies

Beginning about 1850, innovations in mass transportation and communication technologies introduced the Industrial Age.[1] Steamship and railroad companies used electric telegraph systems to complement their delivery of handwritten messages, freight, and passengers from one place to another. Standardized telegraph signaling was made possible by electricity and the invention and widespread adoption of Morse code, through which letters (and therefore words and sentences) designated by short and/or long sounds were transmitted over telegraph wires. This allowed messages to be sent and received nearly instantaneously and in consistently understood ways.

During this time period telegraph messages were sent over wires strung on telegraph poles that spanned long distances between major cities and rural towns. Telegraph companies, such as Western Union, created large telegraph networks often located alongside railroads tracks. In this way, telegraph networks met the needs of railroad companies to signal stop-and-go movements of trains. They also served the larger mass communication needs of a rapidly growing population with expanding commerce.

By 1865, despite widespread destruction in the South during the American Civil War, telegraph operators, called telegraphers, worked throughout much of the United States and Europe. Day and night telegraphers tapped away in odd rhythms on spring-loaded telegraph machines to produce the short and long sounds for messages in Morse code. When the switch was closed (in the "on" position), electric current flowed through a wire. Upon reaching another telegraph machine in a different location, the electric current would trigger an audible signal that sounded like the "buzz" made by a bee. A series of long and short signals were tapped out according to Morse code to create buzzes to represent letters of the alphabet and spell out words.

Telegraphers were experts in listening to, interpreting, and writing down telegraph messages, and also in sending messages along to other telegraph stations just as semaphore station operators once did. After telephones were invented in 1876, operators used telephone along with telegraph systems for all kinds of communications having to do with transporting people, mail, packages, and freight.

By 1900, Western Union maintained one million miles of telegraph lines and two international communication cables under the Atlantic Ocean. Networks of telegraph lines were owned by

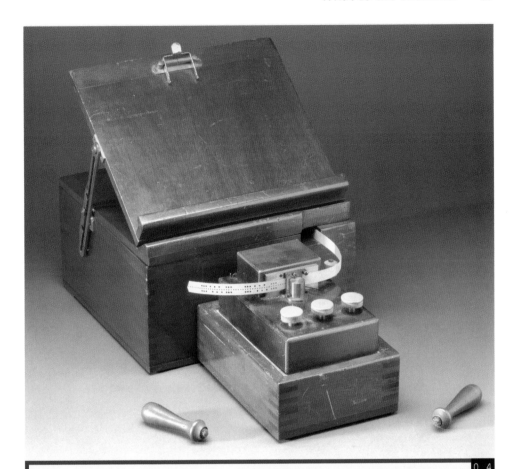

In the 19th century, the electric telegraph was a popular way to communicate quickly and over long distances. Telegraph lines were laid under the oceans, linking every continent together. *(Source: SSPL/Getty Images)*

different companies, however, and new telephone companies such as American Telephone and Telegraph (AT&T) established their own business networks to provide geographically dispersed connections.[2] Within a few more years most American cities had reliable electricity and one in ten American households had a telephone.[3]

Early telegraph and telephone systems often used the same wires, called lines. Early local and long-distance phone lines and services relied on human operators to make electrical switch connections to route messages from one place to another. Operator-assisted phone calls and pay telephone booths remained common well into the 1970s, before computer-automated telephone switching was developed.

From Calculating Machines to Computers

Inventions in transportation and telecommunications technologies ran parallel to and eventually combined with inventions in mathematical calculating machines to set the stage for computers and the Internet. Examples of early calculating machines include:

- The *abacus* used throughout ancient Asian societies. It consisted of beads that could be slid up and down or back and forth on rods to keep track of the things being counted.
- The *odometer*, said to have been used in ancient Greece by Alexander the Great, combined spindles and gears mounted in a wooden box to count revolutions and calculate distances traveled by his armies. Modern cars and trucks use this same basic technology in speedometers and odometers to measure a vehicle's speed and distance traveled.
- The *slide rule* (invented in 1614) operates like two rulers sliding together, with coordinated sets of numbers on each that help users perform mathematical computations. On rare occasions it may still be used by architects, engineers, and scientists to perform complicated math.
- The *adder machine* (invented in about 1650 by Blaise Pascal) combined aspects of the slide rule and the odometer to simultaneously count items of different values. It became the basis for many different kinds of counting devices still in use today.[4]

Early counting and measuring devices could only calculate or save the number of things that people manually kept track of or input in some way, such as by moving beads, turning gears, or sliding rulers. What people really needed was a machine that could automatically process larger amounts of data without relying on human hands.

Progress came with the invention of the weaving loom used to make rugs and clothing. A loom allows an operator to combine different colored thread into beautiful patterns. This is accomplished by using a thread hooked through a wire, which can be inserted into holes to create tightly woven cloth. Manually operated looms are still used in less technologically advanced parts of the world. Few people realize, however, that loom technology (now usually automated with electrical motors and computers) was actually the basis for punch-card machines critical in the development of computers.

In 1725, punch cards were made from sheets of heavy paper or card stock. The cards were perforated with tiny holes in specific places. Hole patterns provided instructions to machines for carrying out tasks repeatedly (i.e., for automation). Punch cards were first used in automated looms to weave patterns in clothing. In 1804–1805, a French silk weaver named Joseph Marie Jacquard invented a loom mechanism that wove patterns of silk on the basis of instructions set out in holes punched into strings of cards. By 1812, more than 11,000 looms were being used in France, and later during the 19th century, other manufacturing processes like packaging, canning, and bottling were all based on automated machine processes powered by steam engines in factories.

In 1890, the U.S. Census was conducted using electric Hollerith tabulating punch-card machines to compute the number of people living in America. By 1937, electrical motors and internal combustion engines largely replaced steam engines to power automated machine processing. This development set the stage for vacuum tubes, transistors, and electronic circuits, all later used in computers which, at this time, were already being conceived for military purposes even as World War II began in Europe.

Fearing the sinking of English and eventually American ships by German submarines, Allied forces were intent on cracking coded messages of the German navy. For this reason, in the summer of 1939, cipher experts met at Bletchley Park in Buckinghamshire, England, which eventually became the British Government Communications Headquarters (BGCH). Among the experts who came was Alan Turing. As a mathematician, he invented an electromechanical machine called the "bombe" that greatly aided in cracking messages sent by Germans who used their famous Enigma encoding machine to encrypt secret messages. In effect, it was machine versus machine in continual battles to encrypt and decipher secret messages in order to sink submarines before they could sink surface ships carrying cargo, troops, or civilian passengers.[5]

During this same period in history Vannevar Bush rose to prominence as an American scientist, inventor, and administrator who had a keen sense of the importance that technology had in matters of national security. During his career Bush made several important contributions to the development of computing. Among his many important inventions and ideas were an analog computer (before digital computing) that became known as the Rockefeller Differential Analyser; and Memex, the notion that individualized storehouses of knowledge could be stored on microfilm and readily accessed electronically through what would become hypertext links.[6] Meanwhile, Howard Aiken was a mathematician, physicist, and inventor curious about using punch-card machines to do arithmetic. His work with International Business Machines (IBM) and Harvard University during the 1940s resulted in the first "information processing machine." It was called the IBM Automatic Sequence Controlled Calculator, or simply "the Harvard Mark I." This huge machine was more than 50 feet long and filled a large room. Punch cards were systematically read (inputted) on one end, calculations were performed in the middle, and results were automatically produced on the other end by electrically powered typewriters. The Mark I was not equipped with a screen for users to "monitor" internal computer processing. Separately connected monitors and printers came about later as did data storage technology such as the portable floppy disk drive.

The first modern computers such as the Harvard Mark I and the Electronic Numerical Integrator and Computer (ENIAC) were used to guide military munitions, rockets, missiles, and eventually spacecraft. These and other mainframe computers of this era were very large machines that relied on vacuum tubes and electromechanical operating technology. Mainframes needed to warm up before they could be used, much like early radios and televisions. Mainframes were also very loud and prone to overheating. They performed calculations and processed data very slowly as compared to modern

IBM's Automatic Sequence Controlled Calculator, also known as Harvard Mark I, is the first automatic digital calculator. Weighing about five tons, it is the largest electromechnical calculator ever built. *(Source: PhotoQuest/Getty Images)*

personal computers (PCs). They also required punch cards created by operators with special programming skills in order to function properly. Consequently, mainframe computers were used only by

PUNCH CARDS WERE ONCE USED TO PROGRAM COMPUTERS

In the early 1960s, before computer monitors were even available, people used simple computer programs like FORTRAN or BASIC to type commands onto 3" x 7" punch cards with many tiny holes in them. The holes punched into the cards appeared in neat rows and columns that corresponded to letters and numbers that had been typed onto the top of each card. By detecting the punched holes, card-reading machines were able to instruct a computer how to carry out a series of particular calculations or perform other kinds of functions. Computer users in those days needed to carefully assemble large stacks of punch cards so that instructions would be carefully followed, one calculating step after another. One slip and dozens of cards could fall all over the place, making it impossible for the computer to understand what to do. To avoid such disasters, punched cards, also called programming cards, were often banded together or stored in an envelope-sized box.

The Hollerith Calculating Tabulator was one of the earliest punch-card machines used for commercial purposes. At a cost of $750,000, the U.S. government used this machine to complete the census of 1890 to calculate the number of people living in America. The process took nearly seven years but was considered a remarkable achievement because more than 50 million Americans resided in the country at that time and counting this many people manually was a daunting task. Other types of early punch-card machines were used to calculate amounts of merchandise in inventories and amounts of money in financial accounts, among other purposes over time.

the military, universities, government agencies, and banks that could afford to purchase, operate, and maintain them.

Throughout the 1950s and 1960s telecommunications and computing technology merged into what today is considered information technology (IT). During these decades organizations other than universities and government agencies began to use mainframe computers. Many companies built electrical appliances used in homes and entertainment devices that resembled boxy furniture. Often called consoles, the entertainment devices of this era combined record players with one-way (receiving) AM/FM radio and television technology.

Consoles provided families with stereo systems that eventually incorporated solid state electronics built only of solid materials and technology precursors of modern digital entertainment centers. The devices were large and operated hot compared to modern personal computers. Today's desktop computers, laptop computers, and minicomputers run cool and are increasingly able to perform faster and accomplish more than consoles and even many mainframe computers from the past. Personal computers are also becoming increasingly affordable, flexible with regard to what they enable users to do, and they are increasingly enjoyable to use.

Unlike old separate electronic devices such as record players, radios, and televisions, modern computing devices are actually miniature self-contained information and entertainment systems. Though small and lightweight, they can process enormous amounts of data very rapidly. Modern computer devices also interoperate on the basis of industry standards. This results in people being able to send and receive data to other people who are using similar devices even though the devices may have been made by different manufacturers.

Modern computers have data input devices such as keyboards or voice-activated software, and other peripherals such as color monitors, Web cams, printers, scanners, and speakers (including headphones). Modern IT devices allow combinations of text, sound, and images to be exchanged online and also off-line by using portable storage devices like external hardware drives, CDs/DVDs, flash drives, and memory cards. Devices also increasingly enable uploading and downloading files to or from the Internet via either wired or wireless connections.

THE INTERNET

The Internet consists of all the computers and digital phones throughout the world that are linked through wires and wireless connections. The Net also consists of information called content posted onto Web sites of the WWW. The Internet and the WWW exist so people located all over the world can share information with

IMPORTANT LESSONS ABOUT TELECOMMUNICATIONS AND COMPUTING TECHNOLOGY

1. Early forms of transportation and information technologies set the stage for computers, other types of IT devices, and the Internet.
2. Major technology developments were made possible by electricity, without which computers, other types of IT devices, and the Internet would not be possible.
3. People have been networked and communicating via wired telecommunications systems for more than 150 years and via wireless technology for nearly a century.
4. Technological inventions and innovations come about as people combine technologies like they did with early telegraph and telephone systems and later with telecommunications and computing technologies.

each other. Since most countries are becoming more computerized, people no longer completely rely exclusively on handwritten messages and postal mail ("snail mail") for sending and receiving messages, nor on printed newspapers and magazines, nor on broadcasted radio and television information to learn about things going on in the world. All these technological sources of information remain important to millions of people. However, Web content enables people throughout the world to leverage Internet infrastructure in ways that are now transforming societies.

The Internet allows people from various countries who have different backgrounds to form relationships and stay connected

Today, IT continues to be infused with many other forms of technology and the Internet to help people in all aspects of their lives.

5. Over time, society adapts to new ways of communicating, but seldom do technologies like telephones and radios disappear entirely from being used. Instead they evolve to become innovative forms of "new technology" that people increasingly adopt into their ways of life.

6. Computerized societies now depend on the Internet for many essential things. Critical information infrastructure for which the Internet forms a technological backbone depends on the generation, reliable distribution, and use of electrical power. However, the Internet and TCP/IP were never designed to be secure, only robust in the event of a nuclear attack. Protecting facilities and information systems that regulate electrical power is a fundamental challenge that governments along with technology, power, and security firms work hard to meet.

with each other, as when they become online friends. Some online friendships last a long time, even for a person's entire life. Meeting people and forming personal or business relationships is a very important aspect of using the Internet and often involves social computing. Checking e-mail, shopping, or chatting online, reviewing news about world events and issues, and doing research for school or work, as well as watching movies, listening to music, and playing games can all be achieved by accessing the Internet and using Web content.

Invention of the Internet

Invention of the Internet occurred over a long period of time. Ultimately it was the result of imagination and much research by visionary thinkers who wondered about possibilities for people using computers to communicate. These visionaries worked in universities and in a U.S. government organization known as the Advanced Research Projects Agency (ARPA). This agency was very involved in supporting computer technology research and development (R&D) for America's space program during the 1960s.

In 1969, ARPA worked with AT&T to connect four dedicated long-distance telephone lines. This experimental network, known as ARPANET, proved that computers could be reliably used to transmit and receive text messages. Over the next few years ARPANET was expanded to link computers located at several additional academic and government organizations. Initially, only computer experts, scientists, and engineers could use ARPANET because most people at the time did not even understand what a computer was.

Beginning in 1972, America's National Science Foundation (NSF) funded more research and development, which led to computers being used by banks, various government agencies, and universities located throughout the country. In 1974, researchers Vinton Cerf and Bob Kahn first used the word *Internet* when writing a paper about how computer data could be sent using a transmission control protocol (TCP). Later, TCP became the technology standard for sending computerized messages over telephone wires.

In 1976, Ethernet was invented, allowing for high-speed transmission of large amounts of data. In this year SATNET (satellite network) was also created as a joint project between the United States and several European nations. SATNET became the basis for using Wi-Fi and cellular phone connections to access the Internet. In 1983, the United States adopted TCP/IP (Transmission Control Protocol/Internet Protocol) as the basis for all Internet connections. This along with creation of the domain name system (DNS) and the uniform resource locator (URL) naming convention for Web site addresses meant that users who wanted to send digital messages did not need to know long numerical IP addresses associated with individual devices. These developments set the stage for use of the Internet and World Wide Web to grow exponentially within a very short period of time.

The Internet and TCP/IP were not designed with security in mind but to withstand a nuclear attack. So in 1984, MILNET (military network) became a separate computer network split-off from ARPANET. MILNET was devoted to sensitive and secret military communications. When the split occurred, the original ARPANET continued to be used publicly, and steadily became known as the Internet. Also in 1984, high-speed, broadband Internet connections were made possible by the telecommunications company MCI, a rival to IBM and AT&T. In this same year Microsoft Corporation released its Windows operating system, which eliminated the need for ordinary users to know computer programming languages.

Beginning in the early 1990s, laptop computers and cellular phones came into widespread use. Microsoft Corporation's development of the Windows 3.0 operating system in 1991, along with improvements in other operating systems and dozens of software applications, made it increasingly possible for millions of ordinary users to enjoy and productively use computers as never before. Windows 3.0 revolutionized computing with a graphical user interface that allowed for visual "click and drag" desktop operations. It also provided icons to open programs and access files located anywhere on a user's computer, on a local area network, or on the Internet.

Beginning in 1993, several Web browser programs, including Mosaic, Yahoo, Netscape Navigator, and Internet Explorer came into being. Browsers allowed users to easily search the Web for content.

The combination TCP/IP, DNS, URL, Windows, and browser technology led to commercialization of the Internet with companies like America Online (AOL) offering users its own ISP connections and content. This approach to expanding online business quickly ended as firms realized that no one company, or even an entire country, is capable of controlling the Internet and all Web content. However, firms like AOL worked hard to provide innovative services to attract customers among increasing numbers of users with Internet access and connectivity. America Online instant messaging (AIM) remains one very popular application and service offered by this firm.

Like MILNET before it, Internet2 became a new network that in 1996 split off from the original ARPANET-turned-Internet. Existing as both a dedicated network (not open to use by the general public) and as a nonprofit organization, Internet2 develops high-performance network applications and technologies. Only people working in certain government agencies, universities, and technology firms can access Internet2. It is like ARPANET when first created, to be used for official purposes such as research that requires high-speed, large-capacity data exchange.

How Big Is the Internet?

The Internet has expanded greatly throughout the many years of its existence and is now the world's primary and largest computer network. In 2011, approximately 2.1 billion people used the Internet. This is about 30 percent of the world's total population (one out of three people). The number of people who use the Net has increased by 480 percent since the beginning of the 21st century. The number and percent of people who have Internet access varies throughout regions of the world.

No one can be sure of how many separate computers and information systems make up the entire Internet. The actual size of the Net changes daily as computer networks are added to the Internet for the first time or are temporarily shut down for maintenance.

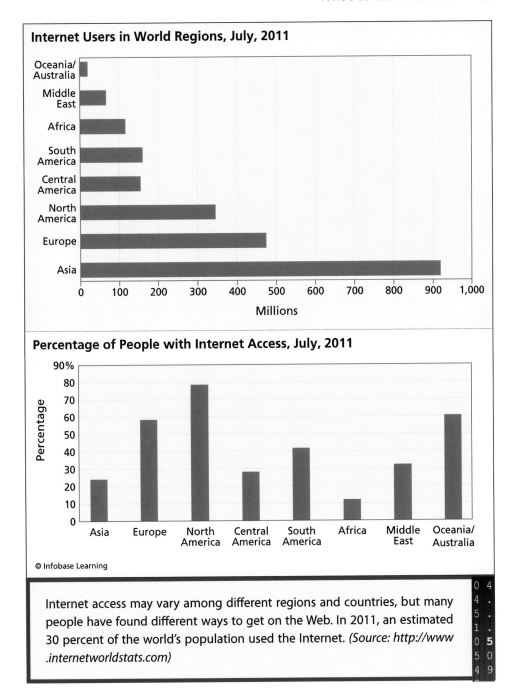

Internet Users in World Regions, July, 2011

Millions

Percentage of People with Internet Access, July, 2011

© Infobase Learning

Internet access may vary among different regions and countries, but many people have found different ways to get on the Web. In 2011, an estimated 30 percent of the world's population used the Internet. (*Source: http://www .internetworldstats.com*)

In 2010, the Internet consisted of more than 160 million Web sites that display content created and posted by organizations and individual computer users.[7] At the time, this was an average of

10 Web pages for every user of the Internet. Since the Internet is growing so fast, it is impossible to keep count or accurately estimate how many Web pages exist at any given time. However, it is correct to think of the Internet as being as big as the planet, larger in fact, because satellites extend the Internet into outer space. Conceivably there are no limits to how big the Internet can become because it is limited only by the number of computers and other IT devices that can be connected, by all the places IT can be located, by the distance light (and therefore electricity) can be transmitted, and by collective information generated in the minds of all Internet users combined.

How the
Internet Works

"Hey Mary, did you add the summer countdown to your Facebook page yet?" cries Sally to Mary as they meet in the school hallway before class. The two girls have been friends a long time and both of them have been using computers and the Internet for more than 10 years. Next week, as they begin high school, both girls will take a computer programming class. They are especially excited to learn about Hypertext Markup Language (HTML) to create or improve Web sites. Mary is known for creating amazing social networking profiles. She already spends much of her free time experimenting with HTML and helping her friends to improve their own Web page content.

The following week Mary and Sally find themselves in the high school programming class. The course instructor, Mr. Miller, explains that numerous programming languages, such as HTML, enable users to create, save, and share documents and content online. Sending and receiving messages over the Internet is usually accomplished with computers installed with e-mail or instant messaging software, or with cell phone text messaging software that is specially designed for this purpose. Mr. Miller goes on to explain that computers, cell phones, and other types of IT devices are known as "hardware" and that IT devices are actually information systems that can be connected to create networks through which data can be sent or received. This was something that Mary and Sally were surprised to learn, though they already knew what Mr. Miller talked about next—that the Internet is composed of billions of IT devices connected to millions of computer networks and telecommunications systems, and that the exact makeup of the Internet is constantly changing and depends on which networks are connected at any given moment each and every day.

Three key things make the Internet possible and allow people to use it:

1. Electricity generated in power plants, supplied through underground and overhead wires, to geographic areas known as *electric power grids* that are located throughout countries and regions of the world.

2. Wired and wireless telecommunications networks composed of computers are controlled by phone and cable companies. They allow people to connect to the Internet using computers and other types of IT devices in order to send (upload) and receive (download) data.

3. *Internet backbones* composed of *fiber optic cables* through which *optical carrier (OC) links* and bands of light now carry the bulk of Internet data. OC links are like major highways that initially carry the bulk of motor vehicle traffic before it becomes routed onto smaller roadways to arrive at final destinations. Optical carrier firms such as MCI and UU Net use a complex technology standard called SONET (Synchronous Optical Network) for data *multiplexing* (i.e., to simultaneously transmit data sent from many sources). Software installed on hardware enables people to communicate with each other

and carry out many other kinds of tasks using data in creative ways.

CREATING INFORMATION AND DATA

People express their ideas primarily through oral and written communication using languages such as English, Spanish, and Chinese. People also express themselves by using IT devices with *operating systems* that are programmed to function with *software* capable of carrying out various tasks such as sending and receiving e-mail. Software is also referred to as a "software application" or simply an "application." Software applications are developed with *programming code* written in a *markup language* such as HTML. Programming code, also known simply as "code," consists of numerals, letters, words, and text symbols combined into logical statements that instruct a device how to process data. Device interoperability is enabled by machine language and programming code standards that allow devices to exchange data when users connect (i.e., "talk to each other").

Computer Languages and Programming Code

The common language understood by all computerized devices regardless of their manufacturer and brand name is *machine language.* This special language uses *binary code*, which consists only of zero (0) and the numeral one (1) written in various combinations and sequences.

Computer devices "read" binary code to switch electronic functions on or off: 1 = on, 0 = off. Early punch-card and computing devices operated on the same principle: A hole in the programming card (or paper sheet) allowed an electrical signal to be completed to indicate "on," whereas a solid space indicated "off." Similarly, computers interpret an electronic signal coded with a 0 to be "off," meaning "NO, do not do anything." However, a program signal coded with the numeral 1, or "on," commands a computer to "YES, do the next thing." When computers read code, they effectively receive a long series of yes or no instructions that guide them through logical sequences of what to do next until an operation is complete.

When used in binary code, 0s and 1s are known as "bits" of data. Computer programmers "write" (i.e., type) binary codes in groups of eight bits. Each group comprises a single byte (of data). Machine data consisting of long strings of bytes looks like this: 11101010 10100110 00100011. Numerous strings of bytes, each having eight bits written in long sequences and lines of machine code, convey instructions that are "read" and interpreted by computers to complete many complicated tasks one logical step at a time.

Programming languages use machine language to convey complex data processing functions. The first computer programming language was called Fortran. It was developed in 1954 by inventors at International Business Machines (IBM) and used in the world's

PROGRAMMING CAN BE FUN AND EASY TO DO

Computer languages vary in how easy they are to learn and use. Programmers use coding languages they understand and that are capable of conveying operating instructions to accomplish specific tasks. For example, a programmer who desires a computer to execute a series of commands in order to print a document in hard copy, or command a robot to complete assembly of parts in a specific order, may use a *general-purpose programming language* such as BASIC, C++, Cobol, Fortran, Java, or Python. However, someone wanting to create or change a Web page will need to use a *markup language* such as XML (Extensible Markup Language) or HTML (Hypertext Markup Language).

Markup languages were developed beginning in the 1980s. Other examples include Scribe, IBM Generalized Markup Language (GML), and Standard Generalized Markup Language (SGML). Social networking Web sites such as MySpace allow users to edit their profiles using HTML coding.

first mass-produced computer, the IBM 650 model computer. Many newer versions of Fortran and numerous other computer languages have since been developed to accommodate special programming needs.[1]

Software Applications

Software applications are computer code that enable IT users to perform many different tasks such as browse the Web, chat, play games online, e-mail, listen to music, or watch DVDs. For every kind of task there are name brand software applications available for purchase in computer stores and online. In addition, freeware and shareware applications voluntarily created by groups of users online

HTML *programming* consists of lines of text that looks like this:

```
<!DOCTYPE html>
<html>
<head>
<title>Hello HTML</title>
</head>
<body>
<p>Hello World!!</p>
</body>
</html>
```

This code includes a variety of "tags" that instruct the computer to perform a series of actions. For example, the first <p> tag in line seven signifies the beginning of a new paragraph. The second </p> tag in the same line ends the paragraph. Text between the tags reads "Hello World!!" When displayed in an HTML editor program, the code would display a Web page with text that says, "Hello World!!" Anyone who uses the lines of code listed above can add this comment to a Web page. Give it try!

provide people with legally free alternatives to purchasing software in stores or online.

The wide variety and availability of software applications today presents a stark contrast to computing in the 1970s and early 1980s. During this period in history and extending into the early 1990s, users were usually confined to using software capable of interfacing with a specific operating system installed on their device. Newer software was not always compatible with older versions of software and vice versa. This situation continues today but to a much lesser extent. Many software developers have improved design and support of applications so that online games and software tools can function across different operating system platforms. This is what allows for interoperability, such as when users use different brands of computers to interact while playing a particular MMORPG (massive multiplayer online role-playing game). Software developers around the world are also helping to expand growth in cell phone usage by designing phone and network-based applications for people of all ages.[2] Advanced "smart phones" are actually minicomputers able to perform many of the same functions that, until recently, only laptop and desktop computers could perform.

By interacting together online, users can write their own customized computer code. When this is accomplished simply for the benefit of users rather than for profit, the resulting code is often made available online for free and referred to as "open source code." Freeware and shareware qualify as open source code. Unless software is open source code and made available to use free of charge, it must be purchased before it can be used legally. Mozilla Firefox is an Internet browser application free to download and use. KeePass is an example of open source software that allows users to manage all their passwords in one place.[3] Whether acquired free or purchased online or in a store, software is easy to download or install onto a computer with a compatible operating system.

TRANSMITTING AND RECEIVING DATA

Sending and receiving electronic messages is what using the Internet is all about. It is easy and can be fun to do with IT devices and

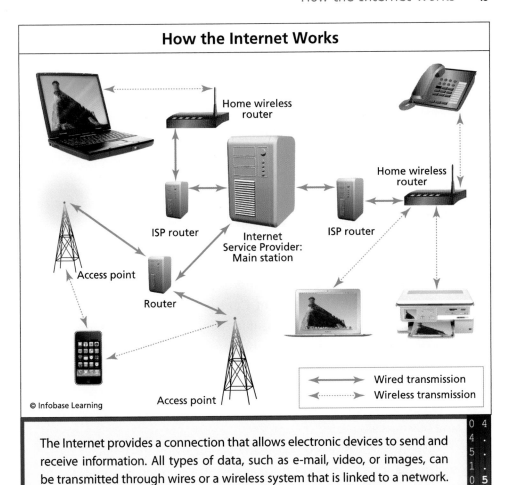

How the Internet Works

Home wireless router

Home wireless router

ISP router

Internet Service Provider: Main station

ISP router

Access point

Router

Access point

© Infobase Learning

→ Wired transmission
⤎ Wireless transmission

The Internet provides a connection that allows electronic devices to send and receive information. All types of data, such as e-mail, video, or images, can be transmitted through wires or a wireless system that is linked to a network.

software. But when a person sends a message electronically what really happens?

An IT device such as a computer or cell phone is used to create and then send digital content over wires (strung between poles or buried underground), and/or wirelessly through the earth's atmosphere (using a source of energy such as radio frequency [RF] waves, infrared light, or laser light). Fiber optic cable used for core Internet infrastructure backbone data transmission is also buried underground. Within a few seconds the message is transmitted through telecommunications networks that are part of the Internet and then received by digital accounts that can be accessed by recipient users. The reliability and speed of data transmissions is determined by several things, including how much data is being sent, processing speeds of devices and networks involved, and atmospheric conditions through which wireless signals must travel. All forms of wireless Internet signals rely on data being able to travel through adverse weather conditions and through or around buildings. Antennae are often mounted on top of tall buildings to help send and receive wireless radio, television, and phone signals.

ELECTRICAL POWER AND NATIONAL ENERGY SUPPLY GRIDS

The largest power outage in U.S. history occurred in August 2003, causing electricity to go out across several Northeast and Midwest states as well as in parts of Canada.[4] This blackout resulted in approximately 55 million people being without electricity for several days. The power outage also caused havoc for other people throughout the world who needed to communicate with those who had lost electrical power. This catastrophe was worsened as people overloaded cellular phone networks in attempts to call loved ones and business associates.

The incident revealed that many people living in computerized societies quickly become confused and frustrated when they lose electricity because it is the source of power for all forms of computer technology. Throughout history telegraph, telephone, radio, television, and computer systems have all required electricity to operate. Without electrical power none of the information systems, IT devices, and the Internet could even exist. But where does electricity come from?

Coal, fossil fuels, and nuclear energy can all be transformed to create heat to boil water, which creates the steam used to drive turbines that generate electricity. Running water, tidal flows, wind, solar energy, and geothermal heat can also be harnessed to spin turbines for making electricity. Most electricity is generated at coal-fired or nuclear power plants. Hydroelectric dams located next to reservoirs or large, fast-running rivers, and wind-powered turbine farms located in windy terrain or at sea also provide much electricity. Once generated, electricity is then distributed throughout regional or national power grids that can be tapped for electricity needed in major cities and rural areas.

Regulating amounts of electricity for use within different power grids is accomplished by people who use computers specifically designed for this purpose. Keeping track of electricity use is especially important during summer months when "brownouts" (periods of reduced electricity) result from people using too much electricity to stay cool with air conditioning. Power spikes or "surges" occur when a grid receives too much electricity, which can potentially damage computers. If power surges are not quickly interrupted, bursts of electricity may exceed the capacities of power transfer stations and short out neighborhood transformers. Brownouts and power spikes cause lights to flicker or go out

In 2003, a massive power outage left regions of the United States and Canada without power. Major metropolitan cities, including New York City, had to find a way to live without basic services such as traffic lights and public transportation. *(Source: AP Photo/Charles Krupa)*

and computers to stop working until electricity is restored. This is why consumption of electrical power needs to be controlled, and why all computers should be plugged into electrical outlet devices equipped with power surge protection.

Supervisory control and data acquisition (SCADA) systems are used to monitor and control processes for distributing electrical power, natural gas, and petroleum products. These computer systems are located throughout regions of the world inside very secure power plants and similar facilities. As nerve centers for providing society with sources of electrical power, natural gas, and petroleum products, like gasoline, SCADA systems are vital to keeping networked computers and the Internet itself functioning nonstop.

TELEPHONE AND CELLULAR PHONE NETWORKS

Using the Internet depends on being able to send electrical-current-carrying signal packets over wired and wireless phone systems. When a person types on a keyboard, a computer interprets the keystrokes as binary code. A variety of programming codes written in a variety of programming languages may be used to enable people to do things online. Phone system switches, routers, and computer servers owned and operated by companies such as AT&T, Verizon, and Sprint, along with Internet Service Provider (ISP) companies, allow users to connect to the Net. When the Internet is working properly, signal transmissions occur within seconds because electricity travels at the speed of light (about 186,000 feet per second, which is 700 million miles per hour).

Internet Service Provider (ISP)

An ISP is a company that provides people with access to the Internet. Methods of connection supported by ISPs include:

1. Ordinary dial-up phone connections (which have the lowest data-transmission speeds)
2. DSL (with incoming data-transmission speeds received from an ISP being faster than data sent from personal devices)

3. Cable modem such as that used to connect digital TVs and phones to the Internet

4. Dedicated high-speed lines that carry data over fiber optic cable lines and satellite cellular phone connections

The type of connection a home, business, or school has determines the speed at which data can be received or sent over the Internet. Dedicated high-speed lines offer the fastest data-transfer speeds and are preferred for downloading music or movies and playing video games online. Data being sent or received over a single dial-up Internet connection or cable modem (commonly installed in residences) will travel more slowly. The types of hardware and software being used also affect the amount of time it takes a device to process a given amount of data. Unprotected computers or cell phones that have acquired malware (malicious software) such as viruses, Trojans, worms, or spyware off the Internet will also operate much more slowly because these programs consume large amounts of data and processing speed time. For all these reasons, and in order to save time and money, businesses, government agencies, and nonprofit organizations often hire technical professionals called system administrators to keep their internal networks operating optimally.

Switches, Servers, and Intranets

A *switch* is an electronic device that connects segments of phone networks in order to route data from one hardware device to another. Switches are located inside devices such as computers and phones, and also in phone companies and connection relay stations located throughout neighborhoods. A *server* is a computer that provides connections with and services to other computers located on a network. For example, businesses often store digital files used by many employees on a server. When one or more employees need to access the file, they can do so by using a computer setup in their own work area or office. Connecting with a server in this way is often accomplished over one or more *intranets*, which are small networks owned and maintained by organizations.

Intranets can be either isolated from or connected to the Internet. Companies frequently use their intranets to enable sharing of sensitive information in ways not exposed to hacking and infection from malware that is so prevalent on the Internet. Large organizations such as city governments use intranets to host various kinds of information about services they provide. For example, a city fire department, parks and recreation department, street maintenance department, and police department may each have separate intranets and Web sites maintained on a citywide government intranet. Intranets are usually available directly to employees,

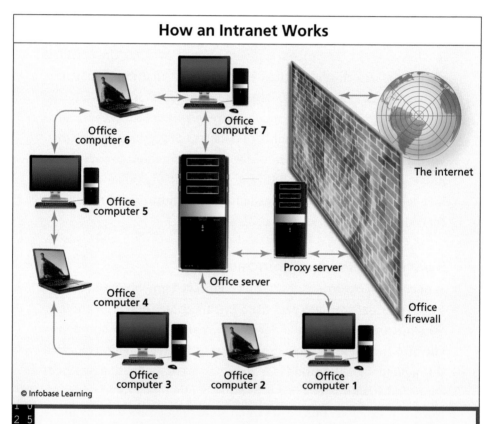

How an Intranet Works

Office computer 6

Office computer 7

The internet

Office computer 5

Proxy server

Office server

Office computer 4

Office firewall

Office computer 3

Office computer 2

Office computer 1

© Infobase Learning

Intranets are relatively small networks that connect computerized devices within buildings throughout organizations and their facilities. Intranets are normally owned, maintained and used by employees and can be connected to the Internet.

THERE IS MORE TO COMPUTING THAN TYPING ON A KEYBOARD!

As a former participant of a pilot laptop program, Tom was given the opportunity to experience how his middle school could integrate computers into the classroom. Every student in seventh and eighth grade was given an IBM ThinkPad equipped with software used in their classes. The school also provided a wireless Internet connection throughout the school building. This allowed students and teachers to engage online while in classrooms, study hall, or the school cafeteria. Initially everything seemed like a great idea. School officials soon realized, however, that many students and even teachers simply did not know how to operate the computers for purposes of classroom teaching or learning about subjects being studied. Most students, including Tom, used their ThinkPads merely to chat with friends, surf the Web, and play games. He was disappointed because he knew there was much more to computing, and he really wanted to learn all he could in preparation for pursuing a career in IT. In addition, failure of the school district to provide technical network support and repair broken computers meant that the entire wireless system, though well intended, caused more problems than it was worth. Within two years the school ended the program. Tom, who loved computing, came to realize that there was much more to using computers than simply turning a machine on and pressing keys on a keyboard.

sometimes from places located outside of main company buildings or facilities. This can occur via the Internet, depending on how intranet switches and servers are configured to operate. Special security arrangements such as creation of virtual private networks (VPNs) can help protect data that is being sent and received through the Internet.

What Is the
Internet Used For?

Jennifer is a sixth-grade student who lives and goes to school in Atlanta, Georgia. One day she told her teacher that a classmate had stolen her wallet, and that she believed Sarah was responsible. When Jennifer arrived home she went online only to find several instant messages from Sarah and other students stating that she was a liar and tattletale. Jennifer wrote back to accuse Sarah of stealing her wallet. Several more messages were exchanged, some from other students who took sides and sent mean messages to one or both girls. The next day the wallet mysteriously showed up on the teacher's desk. It could never be proven who took the wallet or if someone merely found it and returned it to the classroom. Although Jennifer got her wallet back, hurt feelings over the mean messages sent online the previous day lingered and this led the class teacher, Mrs. Johnson, to engage students in talking through many positive and some harmful ways in which the Internet is used.

In the days that followed Jennifer, Sarah, and other students in class came to realize that people use the Internet to exchange information for many reasons. Each day after taking attendance Mrs. Johnson began class by having students discuss ways in which they and their families use the Internet. In the process students reported how smoothly technologies interoperate online. They also discussed how people's online behavior can affect their productivity and enjoyment when using the Internet and World Wide Web. Although most people use the Internet properly to accomplish tasks in harmony with individuals they meet or friend online, a single person or small group of people who abuse others or break the law online can ruin experiences for many others. In the end, the class came to believe that most information sent and received online serves good purposes in education, commerce, finance, transportation, social services, religion, entertainment, and for military and national defense purposes. There is little doubt that society is being transformed by the Internet and World Wide Web.

EDUCATION AND RESEARCH

The Internet and World Wide Web are used extensively in schools by students of all ages. Many elementary schools and nearly all middle schools and high schools are now equipped with computers, many of which can connect to the Internet. Most American children begin to use a home computer to access the Internet when they are of kindergarten age. By the time they enter middle school, nearly all students have used computers and the Internet in classrooms and to do homework assignments.

Classroom activities that involve Web content, watching videos, or interacting online are also increasingly common in school classrooms and libraries. Teachers now commonly use a computer connected to an LCD (liquid crystal display) projector to show Web content to students. High-tech, interactive whiteboards, or SMART boards, enable some teachers to control software applications merely by touching icons projected onto a large screen while computer screen images or Web content is viewed by students in a classroom.

Many schools have integrated digital technology into their classrooms, providing students with the opportunity to use computers, the Internet, and specialized software. *(Source: AP Photo/*Alaska Star, *Melissa DeVaughn)*

The Austin, Texas, Independent School District (AISD) exemplifies ways in which American school districts are now working to increase use of IT and the Internet to support students learning in classrooms. Now in a period of transition "from a fixed desktop approach for classroom computing, to a mobile classroom environment," ASID envisions ". . . reliable, consistent, adequate, efficient infrastructure supporting all mobile computing devices including laptops, netbooks, tablets, smartphones, and other emerging handheld devices. . . ."[1] Future classrooms will each feature a teacher laptop, printer, classroom presentation system, desktop computer and mobile device access for specific class projects. At the district information systems level, AISD is now moving to "cloud computing" to provide teachers and students with shared access to applications formally installed on computer hard drives.

Many computer and software manufacturers are actively involved in promoting use of their products with the Internet in K–12th grade classrooms. Product and service innovations generally pertain to:

- equipping classrooms and enhancing media enrichment centers in libraries and computer labs
- connecting classrooms within school buildings and throughout school districts
- customized "one-to-one" learning strategies that enable teachers to develop lessons and monitor individual student progress

U.S. companies often help American school district officials take advantage of the Universal Service Fund's Schools and Libraries Program that was created through the Telecommunications Act of 1996. Commonly known as "E-rate," this program is the largest and most reliable source of technology funding for K–12 public and private schools in the United States. It provides school districts with substantial financial support from the federal government for local investments to upgrade information technology systems and equip schools with IT devices and the Internet. According to one study, California schools that used E-rate funding realized a 68 percent increase in Internet-connected classrooms per teacher.[2]

The Internet is also used extensively for instruction and research at colleges and universities. Computers enable research to be undertaken in many fields such as astronomy, biology, chemistry, computer and information sciences, health care, and liberal arts such as history, literature, and social studies. Computers used in research are often located in laboratories and connected to machines such as robots and imaging devices that perform a wide variety of technical tasks.

The overall result of information technologies and the Internet increasingly used at all levels of education represents an evolution and revolution in access to information and knowledge that is now greater than at any time in history.

ONLINE SHOPPING, BANKING, AND COMMERCE

Tech-savvy consumers can now locate and purchase an enormous variety of goods and services online without having to walk, use public transportation, or drive to stores. Using a bank card or credit

LEARNING IN SCHOOLS PRIOR TO THE INTERNET

Prior to the Internet and computing, teachers wrote on chalkboards to instruct students. Young students wrote their papers in cursive using only pencils or pens, and older students learned to write using typewriters or word processors. In those days, prior to 1990, it was customary for students to conduct research by only using hard-copy materials located in a library. In the fall, composition books, rulers, and #2 pencils were common on back-to-school shopping lists. Students eagerly anticipated receiving textbooks during their first week of classes because downloading books to read electronically was not possible. Students passing notes in class was also common. Everything was done face-to-face rather than online, and phone access was limited to school offices or lobbies equipped with coin-operated pay phones.

Among the first computers ever used in classrooms was the Personal Electronic Transactor (PET) introduced by Commodore International in 1977. With a retail price of $795 this device came

card, people can shop online day or night as long as they remain connected to the Internet. Many companies like Walmart, Sears, and Barnes & Noble maintain traditional stores in communities but also offer Internet stores. Other retailers, such as Amazon.com, do not have traditional stores located in communities. Rather, they offer products only online. *Online shopping* allows consumers to purchase things not sold in their own community, or in traditional stores, without having to leave their home or another comfortable place in which they enjoy computing. Purchases made online can be shipped anywhere in the world. Online retailers sometimes offer promotions such as free shipping when orders exceed a minimum amount.

with a 6502 Microsoft operating system, 1 megahertz (MHz) processing speed, and 4K of random access memory (RAM). It came with a built-in keyboard, magnetic tape storage cassette and 9-inch, non-color screen capable of displaying up to 40 characters on each line of 25 lines of text.[3] In 1979, two enterprising American 4th–6th grade teachers experimented with a PET to create "interactive programs in weather forecasting, a simulation of the first flight to Mars for Gifted/Talented Child programs and an electronic flip-chart for presentations about computers for schools."[4] During the summer PET access was extended to a total of 20 gifted 7th, 8th and 9th graders who were selected to participate in a two-week "Computer Survival Course for Kids." Adult tutors on the "computer floor" of one school provided assistance to students, several of whom were allowed to take a PET home for one week. By September, at the beginning of the 1979–1980 school year, the school district had acquired 53 PET computers for use in 10 of 13 school buildings. Then, as now, there was concern about how technology could be paid for, how teachers would be trained to use computers in classrooms, ways in which students would use computers to learn, and the potential for computers to be misused.

Online shopping is enabled to a large extent by *online banking*, which allows people to make financial deposits and withdrawals over the Internet. Many workers do not receive paychecks. Instead, they have their pay directly deposited into a checking or savings account. Deposited amounts may then be withdrawn as cash at bank branches or at ATMs, electronically transferred between financial accounts, used to pay bills, or make purchases online. Some merchants allow consumers to receive cash back as a reward after paying for items electronically with a bank or credit card. Free-flowing cash along with money in electronic forms provides for commerce throughout the world.

People must be careful when shopping and banking online. Financial account information must be kept private to prevent criminals from committing online crimes such as *bank fraud* and

The opening of a new Citibank in New York City unveiled interactive sales walls, enhanced image ATMs, free online access, and Wi-Fi for customers. *(Jim Lee/Bloomberg via Getty Images)*

identity theft. Personal identification numbers (PINs), Social Security numbers, and birth dates are very important to keep confidential. Consumers must also ensure that online stores provide for security and protection of financial account data. Fraudulent Web sites can easily be made to look like those of genuine companies or banks, tricking users into entering passwords and sensitive information, which are then captured by thieves. Web sites that depict a closed padlock may indicate a secure source from which to purchase items, although it has been reported that hackers have invalidated this symbol as a guarantee for secure purchasing of goods or services online. Many consumers have been duped in *phishing* schemes designed to trick them into sharing personal information online. Phishing schemes typically use fraudulent Web sites that appear genuine in order to trick people into providing confidential financial account or other personal information. People who shop online, but wish to see an item in person before paying for it, must also be very careful they are not being set up to be robbed in person. Despite such risks, online shopping and online banking are now important aspects of commerce and essential to the economy.

ONLINE ENTERTAINMENT

World Wide Web content provided over the Internet is now the richest and most widespread, accessible source of entertainment in the world. Using computers and certain kinds of portable devices, people can easily download music, movies, or electronic games. After downloading content, it can be viewed, listened to, or engaged in without remaining connected to the Internet. People can also connect to the Net to engage in these and other forms of entertainment in real time through *streaming*, without necessarily saving data to the hard drive of a device. Hundreds of Internet radio and television stations are accessible online through ISP firms and telecommunications companies, such as Time Warner Cable, Inc., which provide entertainment over the Internet for a monthly or "pay per view" fee. The entertainment firm Netflix provides DVD send/return mail service along with video streaming of thousands of movies

TRUSTING ONLINE: BUYING AND SELLING ONLINE WITH PAYPAL

When buying or selling something online, how can people be certain they will receive or get paid for an item? PayPal is a company that specializes in verifying credit card account information used for purchases made online. The company was founded in 1998 by Max Levchin, an online security specialist, and Peter Thiel, a financial fund manager. They obtained $3 million to establish their firm, and initially relied on purchases made from well-known retailers who agreed to pay a small fee to sell items online through PayPal. Buyers also needed to open a PayPal account by providing proof of their identification and a bona fide credit card number. PayPal tracked successful purchases made online, and provided shoppers with sales records and reputations of sellers. In this way PayPal brokered trust between buyers and sellers and helped to promote online commerce. As shopping online became more popular, PayPal expanded its operations to include individuals selling things online. Millions of people now buy and sell a wide variety of items and services online through the service provided by PayPal.

and prerecorded television shows. Many online retailers also sell CDs, DVDs, and electronic games, which once paid for can either be downloaded or shipped to a buyer's location.

A great deal of online entertainment is also available for free. Online users can browse for specific forms of entertainment they are interested in, as well as particular artists and actors. Social computing forums such as Facebook, MySpace, YouTube, and even Twitter, among thousands of other online resources, frequently provide Web links to reviews or popular CD albums and DVD movies. Links to

In 2002, eBay acquired PayPal in a deal valued at $1.5 billion. At the time, eBay was very interested in expanding electronic sales. PayPal handled 25 percent of electronic payments for items sold in auctions, and a majority of sales were still completed via money orders or personal checks.[5] Since that time much has changed in the world of online auctions and shopping. For example, PayPal, as a primary (though not the only) online auction firm, has been hacked. In June 2011, the hacker group Lulz Security claimed to have released account information for more than 62,000 users of PayPal, Facebook, Xbox LIVE, Twitter, and various dating sites. Users living in the United States, United Kingdom, Australia, New Zealand, and Brazil were affected. "LulzSec," as the hacking group is also known, reported that it uploaded the confidential information to a file-sharing site but not before thousands of people "tweeted" to claim having successfully trespassed online to take money from PayPal accounts, change dating site pictures with pornographic images, or engage in chat while masquerading as an authorized account user. A PayPal official explained that confidential information had been acquired through a less secure site and then used to gain access to PayPal accounts. This incident reveals risks that users assume when posting confidential information online, regardless of whether this is done in connection with shopping online.[6]

gaming sites that allow players to compete, make friends, and discover new types and sources of entertaining content are scattered throughout the Web. Browser programs allow all online entertainment links to be bookmarked for easy future reference.

Pirating music, movies, or software means making unauthorized copies of copyrighted or protected content. It is illegal. This means that people who are caught downloading copyrighted content without paying for it may be charged with a crime or sued. Adults who pirate and parents of minors who pirate are increasingly being held accountable and financially responsible for illegally download-ing content. From a legal standpoint, pirating is just like stealing an item from a store, such as a CD, DVD, or gaming software. Tens of thousands of people have now been sued for illegally downloading

MOBILE ENTERTAINMENT

Shopping online for entertainment can be mixed with shopping in person in traditional stores. Redbox, a fully automated, DVD-rental kiosk, now has more than 20,000 outlets located in grocery and convenience stores throughout the country. Kiosk machines are typically located at the entrance to grocery stores and other kinds of retailers frequented by large numbers of shoppers. Machines enable shoppers to view lists of available DVD movies. When a shopper finds a movie to view, they swipe a debit, credit, or other kind of bank card. The DVD can then be removed by the shopper. After viewing the movie the shopper returns the DVD by depositing it in the machine. Redbox rented more than 1 million movies within four months after opening for business in November 2009.

Users of portable IT devices can now choose from thousands of movies to rent online, a process made all the easier with devices equipped with GPS (global positioning system) software to locate a nearby kiosk, browser software to search for and reserve available movie titles, online banking capabilities to provide payment upon pickup (or, perhaps in the future, for immediate downloading and viewing while still on the go). Subscribing members with Netflix accounts can also view movie rental offerings and place DVD orders online using a mobile device. As of this writing, neither Redbox nor Netflix streams movies to all models of smart phones, though Netflix provides streaming to televisions, gaming consoles, desktop computers, laptop computers, some Android phones, and some tablets, such as the iPad.

music. People have also been prosecuted for pirating and distributing copyrighted content without a license or permission. Jail and prison terms are increasingly imposed on violators who are caught pirating. Numerous government agencies, nonprofit organizations, and schools strive to prevent pirating, which can cause huge losses in profits for musicians, authors and software developers, and for companies that produce or publish their works.[7]

TRANSPORTATION AND LOGISTICS

Watching for an expected package to arrive can be like waiting for a pot of water to boil—it seems to take forever. However, the Internet makes it easy for people to arrange for and keep track of things being shipped. Computerization and the Internet have also greatly reduced the amount of time needed to sort and ship things all over the world. In addition, businesses and consumers can sometimes view transportation routes and monitor shipping progress with the aid of online GPS technology. In like manner, passengers equipped with an IT device and an Internet connection can check their travel schedules or progress, whether riding in a car, bus, train, airplane, or ship. Vehicle dispatchers and aircraft control tower operators also use the Internet to communicate with drivers and pilots and to monitor their locations for purposes of scheduling, safety, and security.

GPS navigation systems are an important kind of Internet information system. GPS uses satellites and fixed transponders to provide locations expressed digitally as latitude and longitude. Every place on Earth has a unique GPS location, which allows users to find and keep track of where they are when using a GPS navigation system. The same technology is used by package delivery companies like United Parcel Service (UPS) and Federal Express to tag, route, and track items "shipped" by truck or airplane. Police, fire, and rescue agencies also use GPS technology to locate, dispatch, and keep track of emergency vehicles and personnel. GPS technology is increasingly integrated with 911 emergency phone call systems to enable operators to determine the location of someone in need of help. Military organizations use GPS and the Internet to manage movements of troops and equipment all over the world.

NATIONAL SECURITY, MILITARY DEFENSE, AND SPACE EXPLORATION

The application of computing technology to national security, military defense, and space exploration has dramatically improved such capabilities for the United States and other countries. Military defense once used armor, assorted weapons and munitions, along with ground vehicles, ships, and aircraft that lacked computer-aided technology. With the assistance of computer technology, modern military engineers are able to effectively develop and outfit vehicles, facilities, and soldiers with a wide array of offensive and defensive systems. In general, computerized military technology systems improve: simulator training, communications, transportation, and logistics support for movement of materials and soldiers; monitoring and surveillance of potential threats and targets on land or at sea; deployment of weapons and weapons platforms such as vehicles and soldiers in all kinds of conditions; and accuracy in targeting of missiles, torpedoes, and other types of munitions. Specific examples of computers used in modern military combat operations include the following:

- exploding "smart" bullets or grenades containing distance-calculating microchips fired by a soldier using a handheld weapon such as a rifle or launcher to incapacitate an enemy at a known distance even though they are hiding behind a barrier such as a brick wall
- precision guided missiles (PGMs), also known as "smart bombs," that employ optical, laser, and GPS guidance systems with computer interfacing to identify and acquire specific targets, even while airborne
- unmanned aerial drones like Predator, which is capable of surveillance flights and firing PGMs once specific targets are acquired

Just as modern military vehicles are outfitted with all kinds of high-tech features, combat soldiers today often carry multifunction-weapons systems capable of firing different kinds of ammunition. Soldiers in combat also wear protective body gear that now includes high-tech capabilities for night vision and real-time video transmissions of combat conditions under surveillance or attack. Information transmitted to commanders in arrear of fighting can be used to marshal reinforcements or redirect operations using any combination of conventional radio or high-tech encrypted messaging. Much military surveillance is now accomplished from space with satellites. Nations are also increasingly cooperating to help ensure peace and explore space. Computers and the Internet make this possible.

Modern battle spaces are also experiencing aspects of *information warfare*. Also known as cyberwarfare, network-centric warfare, cyberoperations, or simply "cy-ops," this form of war relies increasingly on information systems rather than primarily on people to carry out combat operations. This idea has existed and been written about since the mid 1990s.[8] It was used to varying degrees in the first and second U.S. Gulf Wars in Iraq and more recently, in certain respects, by the United States to combat potential cyberterrorist attacks and online activities of transnational organized crime groups.[8]

Cyberoperations use information systems to attack the communications, command, and control (C3) capabilities of enemy forces. One particular cy-ops tactic is to launch a distributed denial of service (DDoS) attack in which thousands of computers are remotely programmed to ping servers that control vital information systems. The data overload experienced by the servers effectively shuts systems down. Cyberattacks may also target a national information infrastructure to disable portions of enemy society, such as its Internet hub and communications networks or financial services sectors. In June 2007, "as many as one million computers, mostly hijacked, were involved in the attacks against Estonia's highly developed Internet infrastructure, including government, financial, media and other sites."[9]

For several years the United States and many other countries have reportedly been developing information warfare capabilities.

In April 2005, *Wired* magazine reported that "the U.S. military has assembled the world's most formidable hacker posse: a super-secret, multimillion-dollar weapons program that may be ready to launch bloodless cyberwar against enemy networks—from electric grids to telephone nets."[10] The most recent development occurred in May 2011, when officials at the Pentagon announced that computer sabotage originating in a foreign country could constitute an act of war that could warrant counterattacks using either cyberoperations and/ or traditional military force deployments.[11]

The specter and possibilities for information warfare underscore just how much the Internet has changed how people live and work in defense of themselves, their countries, and ways of life that include using IT devices. Possibilities for information warfare also suggest the importance of protecting critical information infrastructure such as SCADA systems used to control generation and distribution of electrical power. Cyberterrorism and cybercrime present real threats to SCADA systems and many other types of critical infrastructure that people throughout the world now depend on.

From Where
Do People Connect?

Jean lives with her family and attends high school in the city of Chicago. As usual, she awoke to her smart phone alarm clock and although tired, she knew she had to get up and get ready for school. While lounging in bed for a few extra minutes, however, she used her smart phone to connect to the Internet and check for messages. First she checked her personal Facebook page for messages left and then she checked her e-mail account. After responding to several friends, she used her phone browser to check the temperature and weather forecast, information she then used to get dressed in anticipation for her walk and public transit ride to school.

While walking to the nearby city bus stop Jean once again checked her phone for messages. She also visited several Facebook pages of friends with whom she corresponds throughout the day. She noticed a few updates: Mike starts work at 4 P.M., Abby finished her homework but does not think it is very good, and Liz decided to go out again with a guy from a different Chicago high school whom she first met online a few weeks ago.

Once on the bus Jean continues to use her phone to browse the Web for spring fashions, and wonders if working part time on weekends will provide sufficient funds to purchase cool-looking new jeans she has been eyeing. She thinks about how much her combined unlimited calling and data plan cost—about $60 each month—but also about how great being connected is. Suddenly the bus drives into the subway train station tunnel where she transfers. She loses her Internet connection. Just as well. Her battery needs to last until she can recharge in her computer class using a USB port connection.

Portable IT devices have created opportunities for social and mobile computing and transformed how friends, family, and coworkers interact and live their lives. People throughout the world can connect to the Internet from their homes, schools, public libraries, places of employment, or even while they are out shopping or in a restaurant. Depending on available wireless (Wi-Fi) and cellular phone service, people can connect while traveling in a car, on a train, or even while in an airplane. Connecting while on the go is known as *mobile computing.*

CONNECTING FROM HOME

Prior to the Internet, families spent leisure time in their homes playing board games, watching television, reading, or doing other activities. They communicated with each other face-to-face or with people in other locations via telephone or letters. Since the advent of the Internet, various IT devices capable of connecting online have allowed for new means of communication. Today it is common to find a variety of IT devices in most homes, several of which devices may allow Internet access. Devices that may allow for Internet access include desktop, laptop, and minicomputers; TVs; gaming consoles; and mobile devices like smart phones and portable e-book readers such as the Kindle, iPad, Asus Eee, Cool-er, Sony e-Reader, and Barnes and Noble Nook, among others.

The Internet has expanded exponentially over the past 15 years. Computing technology has improved and allowed all age groups

Game consoles and DVD players can connect to the Internet, allowing users to stream videos or surf the Web on high-definition televisions. *(Source: AP Photo/Damian Dovarganes)*

to enjoy its many benefits. Televisions, computers, cell phones, and electronic gaming devices have all grown in capability and popularity with the advent of the Internet. A family room can host an electronic gaming event played not only by members of the household and their local friends, but also by players around the globe. Laptop computers can be used to browse the Internet from the comfort of a warm bed. Friends and family can send text messages and photos to each other using cell phones. Movie nights do not necessarily have to involve going to a theater or a movie rental store but can include streaming movies off a Web site and onto a large projection screen.

USING COMPUTERS AND THE INTERNET IN SCHOOL

The educational system in the United States has evolved over time; however, the concept of education has remained the same, which is the sharing of information, including cultural norms, history, and skills. In the early societies before literacy, education was done orally and through observation and imitation. Parents and extended families taught their children. As cultures evolved and civilizations became more complex, elders began to teach the young skills for agriculture, fishing, construction, and metal work. As a result, the majority of education involved passing on knowledge about occupational tasks. As literacy and the development of writing began, formal schooling developed and later universities were established for the wealthy. Universal education for all children has been a fairly recent development, and it has matured greatly in the past 50 years.

The screeching sound of fingernails on a chalkboard has become quite uncommon with the adoption of computing technology in the classroom, as well as in school libraries and administrative offices. A broad range of positive developments have improved education by utilizing computing technology. First and foremost, educators have added coursework that allows students to develop their interests in fields such as networking, programming, or computer-aided drafting by taking elective courses. Furthermore, some high schools offer basic computing classes in Microsoft Office and Internet research to prepare students for college. Teachers also use computing technology to reach out to their students in new ways. Many students use rapid-fire messaging tools such as AOL Instant Messenger or Yahoo! Messenger or chat rooms to communicate to friends and family. Teachers, especially in well-resourced school districts, have adapted these and other tools such as touch-drag-and-drop Smart boards, multimedia presentation podiums with Internet access that also interface with large-screen LCD projection systems, and so on. Such tools enrich classroom learning environments and engage students in new ways. Some teachers have established Web pages for students to access homework assignments and blogs through which to provide supplemental information related to the class or school activities.

Adoption of technologies in classrooms by teachers relates to financial resources possessed by school districts, age and computer savvy of teachers (young teachers are more inclined to use computer technology), and school policies and curriculum requirements set out by districts in accordance with state and national education standards. Typical state education standards pertain to fine arts, English, language arts, mathematics, physical education and health, physical sciences, social sciences, and technology. Technology standards govern computer and Internet-related knowledge, skills, and abilities that students at various grade levels should achieve. EducationWorld, an online resource for educators, seeks to list these standards for all 50 states along with providing technology-related hints, examples, and resources for teachers.[1]

In the United States and other computerized countries, teachers now recognize the importance of students acquiring *technology literacy*. This concept stresses the importance of students learning all about multimodal communication trends and how multimedia can enhance design and creativity. Also stressed is the importance of students applying information discovered online in ways that benefit themselves and society. Technology literacy also pertains to the need for students to be safe, secure, and ethical when using IT devices and the Internet. All of this relates to how schools are helping students learn how to lead enjoyable, productive, and successful lives in a world that is increasingly getting things done online.

Challenges to using computing technology in the classroom exist. One of the major problems many school districts face is the procurement, implementation, and upkeep of new technology. Installing new computers as well as security and maintenance tools in schools is expensive, and it can be difficult with limited budgets. Once technology is in the classroom, teachers and other staff must be trained, and a technology team must manage and address any security concerns. Such a team must not only be up to date in their knowledge of information technology, but also be able to quickly learn about and adapt to future technologies that can help students and teachers engage in positive learning experiences.

Young people represent an important step in the growth of computing technology. Today it is common to see students enter classrooms carrying laptops, graphing calculators, cell or smart phones, and portable media players or e-book readers. Young people immerse themselves in technology and use their devices to engage in social interactions during the school day, sometimes in ways related to assignments given in class. Sometimes students' use of personal devices in schools raises concerns about using computing technology in the classroom.

Teachers and school administrators often express a common concern: Are students paying attention during school with all of these devices? While some school administrators have banned the use of cell phones and iPods during school hours, others pondered the question and tried to develop less rigid means, such as having students turn off or silence devices during class. Another concern raised is that of plagiarism and cheating. The Internet has provided a new means for students to plagiarize or cheat. For example, some Web sites offer students a service where, for a nominal fee, someone will write a paper for the student. Also, students may copy large amounts of text from online sources and fail to cite the sources in their paper. In response to these problems, other companies offer services that allow teachers to upload students' papers and scan them for potential plagiarism. However, even though these sites offer teachers tools to fight the problem, it is important to teach students the ethical implications and ramifications of using online tools to plagiarize or cheat.

School districts now employ system administrators and information technologists to manage intranets and assist teachers in using computers. Media enrichment specialists also teach students how to use the Internet, and independent groups have been formed to help educate people about technology. For example, kids and adults can learn a lot about Internet safety by accessing i-SAFE, NetSmartz, or OnGuard Online. Web content created by these nonprofit and government Web sites are used in school classrooms throughout the country. They feature games and other content of interest to students, teachers, and parents.

Schools and even classrooms of students now also create Web pages and post content about upcoming events and activities. Sometimes teachers and students use *blogs* to post comments about what they are studying, and teachers can post materials to provide students with assistance on homework assignments. E-mail has become a primary communication tool used by teachers, school administrators, students, and parents. But technology in the classroom is not yet universal. Not all schools provide Internet access or use computers to support learning. Some teachers who grew up without computers have difficulty using IT devices to enhance classroom instruction. Consequently, students accustomed to using IT devices outside of school may not be engaged to their full potential in classrooms that lack computing technology.

COMPUTER USE IN THE WORKPLACE

Technology has long played an important role in how products and services are produced and offered to consumers. In the 18th and 19th centuries, factories were built in the United States, England, China, and other countries to produce goods and centralize work previously done by many small artisan shops. As years progressed, technology evolved to improve factory efficiency and the overall quality of goods produced. In the early 20th century, Henry Ford became famous for use of the assembly line for mass production of automobiles, in which workers stood alongside a series of rolling ramps that convey the parts needed to produce cars. The assembly line spread to many other industries, and the increased efficiency it created helped bring down prices of many types of goods, including prices of electronic and computer products. Beginning in the 1970s, industrial robots that could do some tasks faster and better than people appeared on assembly lines to further improve factory productivity. Today the greatest influence comes from computing technology, which has evolved to affect millions of employees working at various jobs in many industries as well as in government, business, nonprofit, academic, construction, transportation, and other employment sectors.

Most people now use computer technology every day at their job, sometimes in ways they may not even realize. Activities, such as correspondence, record keeping, and research, are performed using computers, as are jobs that involve computer-aided design (CAD), manufacturing processes, and tracking of packages shipped from manufacturers to stores or consumers. Often computer technology is embedded into tools, equipment, and machines. Modern cars and trucks are controlled with computer systems built into engines, transmissions, and electrical systems. The same goes for trains, airplanes, ships, and large earth-moving equipment such as bulldozers. Robots used in factories and tall construction cranes used to build buildings also rely on computerized control systems that help ensure worker productivity and safety. Computers are also used in farm and agricultural equipment, commercial fishing, and in emergency services provided by police and fire agencies. For example, tractors and combines now used in agriculture may be equipped with GPS technology that interfaces with satellite geo-imaging of field moisture and soil conditions to guide automated planting of seeds to bring about enhanced crop yields. Similarly, commercial fishing vessels use GPS and ocean thermal imaging technology to locate water temperature depths and currents favorable to particular species of fish. Police, fire, rescue, and other emergency services

THE E-ZPASS TOLL COLLECTION SYSTEM

Jobs everywhere have been affected by computing technology. Simple tasks that were once done by people are now automated through computing technologies. Computerizing jobs that people once did affects the number of employees at companies or organizations as well as productivity. Many states in the northeastern United States, for instance, now use the E-ZPass system to verify that vehicles passing through a toll booth location have prepaid the toll. Drivers of vehicles with prepaid E-ZPass devices are "green lighted" through checkpoints without having to stop to manually pay the toll. This electronic toll collection system is based out of New Jersey, yet controls monitoring stations on roadways in several Mid-Atlantic states. Installation of the E-ZPass computer system decreased the number of toll booth operators needed to collect money from drivers. Similar systems are used in other regions of the country. Although studies about job losses experienced by toll booth operators are not currently available, in March 2011, unionized New Jersey E-ZPass employees staged complaints over impending layoffs and demanded that state civil service officials negotiate alternatives to layoffs. A blog that recorded people's reactions to the situation showed that most were insensitive to toll booth operators, who reportedly earned relatively high salaries and benefits for what many bloggers considered to be low-skill and obsolete employment.[2] While many toll booth operators may lose their jobs, especially during economically difficult times, it is doubtful that all of these employees will be replaced anytime soon because of the many human requirements that toll booth operators perform, such as collecting money (from toll machines as well as drivers), giving motorists directions, reporting violators, facilitating violation investigations, and helping to maintain toll booth facilities.

professionals also use computers for dispatching and monitoring incident locations in relation to response unit availability. The Chicago Police Department maintains a central communications and dispatch center that utilizes several enormous screens capable of displaying maps of city regions and the locations of available and occupied emergency vehicles and personnel.

Professionals in fields including medical, legal, research, educational, and other human services also use computers on a daily basis. For example, doctors have begun to use iPhones to assist them in viewing medical images and prescribing drugs for their patients with the software application Epocrates. This app enables doctors to check possible side effects and potential reactions that could occur if certain prescription medicines are taken together. Lawyers commonly use a database called LexisNexis to research laws and legal case precedents. Similarly, researchers often use Google Scholar as a means of finding out about completed studies in all sorts of fields. Teachers now use Web content and a variety of online teaching tools to aid in their classroom instruction. And human service professionals use computers, IT devices, and also the Internet to access information needed to help people in routine and emergency situations. Many health care, emergency response, and other human service workers now respond to incidents by carrying portable devices that enable them to record case notes, complete standardized forms, draw diagrams, communicate with their dispatcher or office, and access the Internet to obtain information related to the case circumstances they are managing.

Although computer technology and the Internet have encouraged advancements in many areas of society, computerization is not without negative effects. Computers have caused many people to lose jobs. For example, some retail stores have replaced cashiers with self-serve checkout stations that invite shoppers to scan their own purchases and pay without human assistance. Many unskilled but technical jobs are especially vulnerable to being changed or replaced through computerization. Many industries have experienced decreases in the number of available jobs because of computerization. Some fields,

Smart phone users can download apps directly onto their devices. Many corporations develop apps to provide more information on their products or extra services to their customers. *(Source: PRNewsFoto/Pfizer Inc.)*

however, have seen increases as computer technology has created a need for new types of workers. A good strategy for students today preparing for future jobs is to become proficient at using computers and other types of IT devices that are increasingly relied on throughout society.

MOBILE COMPUTING

Joan Allen is a social worker who often works in the field meeting with people to discuss their living situations and the benefits programs for which they may qualify. Two years ago, her employer provided her and fellow social workers with a portable computer. The device features a flip-up, rotating screen that allows her to input information using a touch-screen stylus. From the field Joan is able to fill out standard case file reports and forms, check her e-mail, and go online to check out information related to personal circumstances of her clients.

Last summer Joan purchased an iPhone with an unlimited calling and data plan. She uses the device every day for personal or work-related activities, such as making phone calls, checking e-mail, texting, updating her Facebook page, browsing the Web, checking out YouTube videos, and for listening to music, watching movies, or playing electronic games. Joan finds that having both the laptop and her iPhone enables her to fully enjoy the benefits of mobile computing. Having both devices in the field while working maximizes her flexibility and ability to be productive. However, Joan understands that using the devices for personal reasons can interfere with her professional obligations, so she keeps her personal and social computing activities during work hours to a minimum.

Millions of people now use portable IT devices for the same kinds of activities. High-tech smart phones such as iPhones, BlackBerries, and Droids, among many other brands of devices, empower people to engage simultaneously in social and mobile computing. What can be done with the devices is limited only by a growing number of apps that can be purchased and the availability of peripherals such as earbuds or headsets. New functions such a voice recording, video and still cameras, and GPS are increasingly being built into smart phones

TEENS KEEPING UP WITH TECHNOLOGY

Young people are especially prone to wanting the latest technology device available. Such desires may naturally have to do with curiosity, being technologically challenged, increasing knowledge and skills, measuring up due to peer pressure, or showing off for friends. In general, teens are thought to be more knowledgeable than their parents about technology, but they usually depend on parents for financial support in purchasing devices and maintaining calling or data accounts. Here are examples of two teens wanting to keep up with newer technology:

Spoiled 16-year-old

"I have had nine different phones in the past three years. I always want to have the best phone among my friends. When the iPhone came out, I had to have one so I went with my parents to stand in line with everyone else. Just recently, I got the Droid from Verizon. My parents had to pay a couple hundred dollars just to cancel our AT&T contract to use the iPhone before I could use the Droid through Verizon. How could they say no to my having the best phone made? They need to make sure I have a device I can use in case of emergency!"

17-year-old mobile gamer

"I bought my most recent phone so I could download games and apps. When my mom went to use the phone it took her 10 minutes just to figure out how to call someone. She got angry because she couldn't understand why it took so much effort to call someone on a phone. I told her, somewhat falsely, that cell phones are not used for calling people anymore—most people text and game."

to allow users to be very creative in the kinds of content they create and to keep track of their location.[3] Users can also use these devices to check the weather, shop online, send virtual greeting cards, look for restaurants or other kinds of stores in a given geographic area, update their calendar, and more. People can use applications on cell phones to upload pictures to Facebook or MySpace and update their profiles. Twitter is another popular service that allows its users to update their status at a moment's notice and while on the go using their cell phone or laptop.

Regular use of cell phones is common among young people and adults. Many people have replaced home-based telephones with cell phones so they can communicate and check messages from home or while on the go. In 2009, there were 4 billion mobile phone subscriptions, more people had camera-phones than all computers of any kind, and short message service (SMS) text messaging was the most common function used on cell phones and smart phones and worth more than $130 billion in telecom services.[4] For many young people, texting has become so accepted that they have no problem texting rather than speaking to someone, even if they are sitting, standing, or walking right next to the other person.

Social Computing

When you're little, everything the "big kids" have looks way cooler than anything you do. Easy-Bake Ovens are nothing compared to anything that Apple makes. Toy cell phones look stupid next to someone's BlackBerry. And drawing your ideas and thoughts in chalk on the sidewalk doesn't get the same response as a Facebook update, a Tumblr blog, or a tweet to all of your followers. And asking questions of your parents will simply get you an in-depth answer that you don't want, a blank face that tells you they don't know what you're talking about, or "go ask someone else" versus the quick response of Google. Then, of course, once you're one of those "big kids," social computing concepts become an obsession. Of course this is not true for every teenager. Maybe you only use certain social networking sites, maybe you don't text people, and maybe you do everything that there is to possibly do on a smart phone, assuming you are lucky enough to have one.

We all know these things can do pretty much anything you want. At 7 A.M., alarm is ringing. Get up. I can't really tell what the weather is going to be so I check it with my phone. Then check Facebook. How many comments did I get on my newly uploaded profile picture? Friend requests. My ex-boyfriend, my gym partner (why were we not friends!?), my neighbor's mom, and my lab partner's iguana that he hides in his backpack . . . random.

Eat breakfast and check e-mail at the same time. Call mom on the way to work with the Bluetooth in the car. Call boyfriend and remind him he has a doctor's appointment at 9 A.M. Get to work, check e-mail again. Sit as a receptionist and handle everyone that comes in the door. Naturally, if there are no projects, my mind wanders. Read PerezHilton.com and OMG, two celebrity gossip blogs. Log onto Tumblr. See what my friends are blogging about. There's music, their interests, re-blogging something that someone else blogged. Then I re-blog some of the things that they've blogged. And then I blog about people who come into the office trying to give me a hard time because they need to see someone they did not have an appointment with. I can only offer them an appointment later in the day. My post is angry. More re-blogs.

Take a picture. Title it "NEED CAFFEINE" and upload to Facebook. Coffee break! Joke. Decide to tweet that and see what people say. Back to work. Check e-mail. Someone sent me a video from YouTube. It's of this girl singing, how not unique. Oh wait, she's got a legit record deal from this thing. Google "Rebecca Black." Results = insane. Spend 20 minutes reading about Rebecca Black. Update Facebook status, "I have 'Friday' by Rebecca Black stuck in my head and I love it." Check Twitter to see previous comments and tweets. Lots of sympathizers. Check Facebook, whoa, my friends are being mean to this poor girl and dislike my status a lot. Update status, "I love Google." Instant likes on my status. More work. Text BFF Jill and see if we're still on for lunch. Check someone into the office. Get a text saying, "YES! So in." Send texts for lunch plans. Then remember to text work friends for a movie one night. Text other friends for outfit plans for laser tag.

Work is over. Go home. Try not to look at phone. Get home and log onto computer. Check Facebook. SO MANY NOTIFICATIONS.

Comments on profile picture, pictures from last weekend, all of today's statuses, some of yesterdays, and videos I posted on other people's walls. Go to news feed, read everyone else's statuses. Like some, ignore others, text friends about a girl I don't like but how someone else likes her status but I'm not gonna like it because then she'll think that we're friends. Skype message! My friends want to video chat. Video chat and search Google and Facebook all at the same time. My Skype messenger is blowing up because I haven't checked it all day. Chat messages and a video message with friends.

Log onto YouTube, pull up my favorite music video. Play video, then share the screen with my friends so they can see everything on my screen. Facebook, stalk my crush while still sharing the screen. Stop sharing screen as soon as I see the changed relationship status. I instantly see my friends typing on their screens. They've found it too. All of our faces look so dejected. Wait. Screen shot of all our faces to remember this moment and how funny the faces look. Open Google again, this time search "summer hairstyles." Find the perfect one. Screen share again and get everyone's opinion. Perfect, now how to do it. Google. Find the "how to." Try it. Show friends. Get approval. Upload pictures to Tumblr and blog about how great summer is because there are shorts and new hairstyles that are perfect and summer dresses. Upload pictures of all of these things. Notice that people have re-blogged my blogs. Smile. People like my thoughts. 11:30 P.M. Well, that was a day. No homework but lots of social computing. Go to sleep while texting. Think about all the social interactions there will be tomorrow, all through the Internet

Communication allows for the transfer of information among people. Humans have always been interested in sharing information and have done so either orally or in writing. Through communication people built relationships and thus developed cultures in which they shared similar values and interests. Prior to the Internet, people communicated through postal services, then via telegraph and telephone, and later radio and television. Newspapers, magazines, and academic journals also provided ways for people to communicate and stay informed, as did cork bulletin boards upon which announcements and messages could be posted. The Internet has supplemented all these ongoing means of communication by merging computing and telecommunications technologies. This in turn has allowed people to communicate, associate, socialize, and organize in new ways. In the process, geopolitical boundaries separating people are becoming less important while online markets through which people shop and trade for goods and services are becoming increasingly inseparable. All of these changes are taking place through a phenomenon called social computing.

WHAT IS SOCIAL COMPUTING?

Social computing has to do with people using wired and portable IT devices to interact with each other online. It is enabled by information systems that support gathering, analysis, representation, or dissemination of data among people who associate with each other in groups, organizations, communities, and markets. The potential power of social computing rests in information not being anonymous, but rather linked to individual users and the people to whom they in turn are linked. Social computing encompasses e-mail, texts, blogs, online gaming forums, personal profiles, tweets, or any other computer-supported technology medium such as YouTube that allows people to identify and express themselves while interacting with or "friending" others online. Social computing can be used for both personal and professional purposes. Many working adults maintain professional profiles on Facebook, LinkedIn, or similar social computing services. Social computing is also an evolving phenomenon that organizational leaders, technologists, and researchers are trying to better understand and leverage for all sorts of purposes.

Social Computing and Media Firms

Social computing firms are companies that specialize in helping users with similar interests or backgrounds to connect with each other online. Social computing firms that allow users to create profiles include Facebook, LinkedIn, and MySpace, among many others. The social computing firms that facilitate users connecting with each other online include firms such as Twitter and YouTube. Telecommunications firms such as Verizon, AT&T, and Sprint also qualify as social computing and social media firms because they facilitate people connecting online. Content providers such as America Online (AOL), which also provide e-mail, instant messaging, and Internet gaming, also qualify in this category. AOL was one of the first companies that offered its customers the opportunity to create an online profile. Users could include their name, age, location, and personal interests. This information then could be shared with other AOL users and people could search the AOL profile database to find new friends or reconnect with old friends.

It is difficult to pinpoint social computing and media firms because a majority of companies now maintain a Web presence that may include online interactions with customers, clients, vendors, shareholders, and the general public. In addition, many firms now employ an "online community manager" or a similar professional to provide guidance for improving social computing and media-related services and to help firms to remain competitive in the digital age.

Since the beginning of the 21st century, computerization has expanded greatly through use of mobile computing combined with social computing. There is simply no question that the ability to carry around a smart phone, along with a laptop or minicomputer, has changed the ways in which people live with the Internet. Companies have reinvented themselves to take advantage of mobile and social computing, and even entirely new industries are making possible rapid changes in how information systems and IT devices work together seamlessly while bringing together different types of media and content. Nowhere is this more evident than in the entertainment industry.

The most famous digital music and content application is iTunes, which is run by Apple Computer, Inc., the company that makes Mac computers, iPods, iPads, and iPhones. The app, released

Members of Facebook or MySpace can use these social networks to reconnect with old friends or long-lost relatives. Facebooks users can communicate through private and public messages or, with a webcam, through video
calling. *(Source: AP Photo/Charles Rex Arbogast)*

in January 2001, allows users to connect to the iTunes stores "to
purchase and download music, music videos, television shows,
iPod games, audiobooks, eBooks, podcasts, feature length films
and movie rentals." Users can then use iTunes to organize playl-
ists of entertainment content to listen to and/or watch while using
an Apple device such as an iPod, iPad, or Mac computer. Users
of iTunes can also use the app to listen to and watch Internet TV,

listen to radio or podcast shows, and shop in the iTunes store for thousands of other kinds of applications to do a myriad of other things. Devices with an Apple logo and white earbud listening cords worn around by users are a sure sign they are a fan of iTunes.

Spotify is another online media company that allows users to select various types of music. Selected tunes are then streamed over the Internet to people using a computer or smart phone. Spotify runs commercials to support broadcasting, making it essentially a new form of radio broadcasting and a computer experience that is very different from merely listening to an AM/FM radio at home or in a car. A quick Web search for Internet radio companies or radio stations will produce long lists of possibilities through which varieties of music can be heard online without long interruptions for hours at a time.

Users can now also choose from a variety of Internet TV applications and services, many of which are viewable on portable devices such as smart phones. For example, for a one-time fee (of approximately $50 in 2011), SPB-TV can be downloaded and used to access more than 150 subscription-free TV stations broadcast online from around the world. Stations such as TV Pampa, which broadcasts from Rio Grande do Sul, Brazil, feature news, musical shows, interviews, cooking shows, and more. Nation-specific news can also be ascertained via stations such as Austrian broadcast HT1 Hausruck TV Live, or France 24, or China's CCTV, which also offer business, sports, and cultural reports. More focused channels such as NASA feature scientific and educational programming; CBN features Christian world news; Comedy Time features urban, Latino, and mainstream stand-up comics; and Massive Bike TV is all about biking activities, sports, and lifestyle.

Netflix, Redbox, and Blockbuster are also companies that specialize in delivering digital entertainment content, specifically movies. These businesses offer low-cost rental and/or monthly membership fees for which they provide in-store pick up of DVDs, quick delivery of DVDs to a person's mailbox, or streaming video online. Cable television firms such as Time Warner Cable, Inc. stream movies and TV show content to a user's computer, smart phone, TV via a Wii, PlayStation 3, or Xbox 360, or other devices. Typically subscribers have extended periods during which they can view content rented in stores, online, or received through the mail.

SOCIAL COMPUTING FORUMS AND USER ACTIVITIES

There are many ways in which people can engage in social computing. Methods and types of forums include Web site communities, blogs, YouTube, online gaming, instant messaging, texting, and e-mail.

Web Site Communities

Online communities on the Internet allow individuals across the globe to come together and share stories and express themselves. These communities form around shared interests or are based on culture. There is an online community for every type of person, and if not, a person can easily create a group to find new friends. For example, Yahoo! Groups allows users to create or join online forums, groups, and communities. A quick online search reveals unlimited opportunities for social computing in many subjects of interest such as animals, computers and the Internet, entertainment and arts, health and wellness, music, recreation and sports, and school and education, among many other more specialized subjects. Yahoo! also provides users with an online dating service (Match .com on Yahoo!), a new- and used-car consumer advice and finding service (Yahoo! Autos), updated stock market and other financial information (Yahoo! Finance), and Flickr, which allows people to upload and download photos in connection with other social computing activities. Through Yahoo!, users can also easily search for jobs, real estate, and stay apprised of who celebrities are and what they are doing (OMG! from Yahoo!). On its homepage Yahoo! also features icon buttons for games, horoscopes, movies, Facebook, and Twitter, among other things. Featured partners buttons provide direct links to Netflix and the University of Phoenix. In these ways, Yahoo! exemplifies methods in which modern media firms can simultaneously promote and leverage social computing and the Internet.

Two other general and very popular, current social networking services are Facebook and MySpace. Both of these services offer people the ability to post pictures, videos, personal information, and blogs, and to send messages to one another. While these sites offer their services to all age groups, young people comprise the highest percentage of users. Users "friend" each other to add people to their list of online friends. Some users have hundreds and even thousands of online "friends" even though they may actually know only several or a few dozen people in the traditional face-to-face sense. It is common for some users of MySpace and Facebook to spend countless hours on these sites to update their profiles and communicate with friends all the while accessing many other Web sites and social computing forums.

Other social networking sites allow people to find friends based on their interests or promote networking for employment opportunities. LinkedIn allows people to interact and add each other to their professional association network based on prior and present relationships. Employers can view LinkedIn Web sites to determine if a candidate is qualified for a position based on the people and organizations with which they associate.

Blogs

A blog is a type of Web site typically developed by one or more individuals on their own behalf or to benefit a cause or organization. Blogs involve personal commentary about life events, news, politics and so forth, and may include text, audio, or video content. Many blogs are sponsored by companies or organizations for marketing or publicity purposes. People who host or participate in blogging are called bloggers. For some bloggers, blogs offer a new way to journal personal thoughts and experiences. However, blogs can also allow friends or the general public to post comments. Today, journalists in

A CLOSER LOOK AT FACEBOOK

Facebook is a social networking service and Web site that is operated and privately owned by Facebook, Inc. It was launched in February 2004 by Mark Zuckerberg with his college roommates and fellow computer science students Eduardo Saverin, Dustin Moskovitz, and Chris Hughes. The Web site was originally intended only for students of Harvard University in the tradition of creating an annual "face book" of students, faculty, and staff. However, Facebook soon broadened its availability to all Internet users over the age of 13 with a valid e-mail address.

In Facebook, users create profiles that typically include descriptions of themselves and their interests. Profiles also include photos and are often updated with personal news and comments. Users can add friends, send messages, and update privacy settings along with profile information to notify friends about what is going on in their lives. Additionally, users can join networks organized by workplace, school, or college attended.

Facebook is among the most popular of all social computing platforms. With more than 750 million active users in September 2011, the influence and effects it has as the world's largest social computing network are hard to overstate.[1] Influences that Facebook has on the thinking and behaviors of people extend far beyond friends merely meeting online and sharing music. In 2011, a journalist observed a situation in which his brother's friend met a young

the media and subject-matter experts use blogs to post information about current events and controversial issues, many of which are then responded to by members of the public. Many so-called blogospheres exist to support online discussion about current political, legal, medical, social, and other types of issues.

lady at a bowling alley. They spent a few hours together socializing, after which the friend asked the girl out to dinner. The girl said, "I don't go out with anyone unless I'm friends with them on Facebook, so friend me on Facebook!" She was not making excuses. The friend took her out to dinner but only after friending her on Facebook.[2]

Facebook users generally post tidbits of information about themselves in streams of thought that pertain to their feelings, relationships, and activities. Individual profiles allow users to create and customize content that is as unique as they are. In posting content and updating frequently, users can write, photograph, and videotape themselves into existence and reshape public branding of themselves with respect to friends and interests in remarkable ways.

This means that personal profiles can also be used as an "e-portfolio" for purposes of marketing professional talent to prospective employers as well as expanding social networks. Increasingly, college and even younger students are leveraging their ability to create clever profile content to feature special knowledge, skills, and accomplishments that organizations may find attractive. The reverse is also true: Colleges and employers are increasingly checking out users' online profiles to discern talents of prospective students or employees. For this reason users should be creative and also cautious about the kinds of information they provide about themselves online or post to accounts of other users, and they should make sure that content is favorably updated before applying to college or seeking a new job.

As of December 2007, blog search engine Technorati was tracking more than 112 million blogs.[3] Blogging has become a popular daily activity among young and adult users of the Internet. Companies like LiveJournal and Blogspot offer free blogging tools and space for bloggers. However, millions of independent blog sites exist and blogging services are also commonly made available by social networking sites such as Facebook and Twitter.

YouTube

YouTube is a Web site and social computing community in a category of its own. Here users can upload and share videos of varying lengths and containing content ranging from mild and humorous to violent and adult-oriented. YouTube functions as social computing because videos posted by users as art and content express points of view about diverse subjects sometimes interactively, as when videos are posted in response to other videos.

YouTube was developed in 2005 by former PayPal employees and in 2006 was bought by Google. Users do not need to register for the service; however, if a person decides not to register, they are limited to only viewing certain videos, while registered users can upload videos. Content is restricted if it contains explicit sexual content and only users that are of age and registered may view it.

Verification of age is not routinely done by the firm. Rather, users upon registering for an account are prompted to declare their age. In addition, terms of agreement include age-related advisories that, in part, state that some content is intended only for adult viewers at least 18 years of age, and that YouTube is not intended for people less than 13 years of age. Younger users are encouraged to access other Web sites and confer with parents about what is appropriate to view online.

While the majority of the content that is available on YouTube is content that has been uploaded by individual users, companies such as CBS and BBC have also uploaded their material for individuals to watch. Some of the content includes commercials, television shows, and movie trailers.

Online Gaming

Online gaming is an activity that millions of people across the globe enjoy, and some commit seemingly endless amounts of time to it. Online gaming has evolved from forms of traditional nonelectronic games. It consists of using an electronic device to access the Internet to interact with a game program. There are many types of online games. Among the most popular types are: first-person shooter (FPS), adventure, massive multiplayer, real-time strategy, role-playing games (RPG), and turn-based strategy. Massive Multiplayer Online Role-Playing Games (MMORPGs) are essentially adventure-RPG games that are entirely based in an online environment. In these gaming environments players typically assume the role of a character or avatar that represents them in some manner. Most, but not all, online games consist of multiplayer interactions. The number of players varies among online game titles, and unity often exists among gamers who play the same game.

Thousands of games are for sale online and in traditional gaming stores. Games can be installed locally to a player's machine, but game players can also connect via broadband or other network connections to a Web server to play. The primary purpose of the game is often character interaction, having players work together to solve puzzles or complete "quests" for experience or power-up items.

Video game sales are overtaking music media sales, and are expected by 2011 to exceed $50 billion dollars in value.[4] *World of Warcraft* alone is estimated to host up to 3 million players at any given time and has more than 11 million monthly subscribers worldwide.

Internet addiction, crime, and violence are often associated with excessive online gaming, but social scientists, policy makers, parents, and gamers themselves disagree about this and other controversial matters related to gaming. On June 28, 2011, the U.S. Supreme Court struck down a 2005 California law that banned selling of violent video games to minors. In authoring the high court's 7-2 decision, Justice Antonin Scalia wrote, "Video games qualify for First Amendment protection. Like protected books, plays, and movies, they communicate ideas through familiar literary devices and features distinctive to the medium. And the basic principles of freedom of speech . . . do not vary with a new and different communication medium."[5] One concerned gaming industry executive reacted to the decision on a blog by posting, "Everybody wins on

A visitor to the world's biggest high-tech fair, the CeBIT, plays *World of Warcraft*. MMORPGs like *World of Warcraft* provide an online environment that allows people, through the use of avatars, to interact with users from all over the world. *(Source: Nigel Treblin/AFP/Getty Images)*

this decision—the Court has affirmed the Constitutional rights of game developers; adults keep the right to decide what's appropriate in their houses; and store owners can sell games without fear of criminal prosecution."[6]

Instant Messaging, Texting, and E-mail

Businesses, governments, nonprofit organizations, academic institutions, and individuals now also use instant messaging, texting, and chat rooms to communicate and socially interact online. Instant messaging is accomplished with computers. Texting, which is essentially the same thing, is done with cell phones. Both forms of communication involve creating and sending short messages in real time. They allow for rapid-fire messaging between users.

People may engage in multiple, simultaneous conversations. They may also use voice, file transfer, video connect, and game play services in concert with instant messaging or texting services. Users may set their program to log, or automatically save, each text-based message. Each person creating a screen name may also create a profile that users may view. Buddy lists of friends helps to identify the group of people with whom a user often communicates. A person receiving a text or instant message may reply according to provisions of their ISP or data use plan. Texting is now done directly from cell phones and smart phones; AOL, ICQ, Yahoo! Messenger, and Trillian remain popular instant messaging clients in instances when users engage in texting with computers or smart phones.

The Internet now allows a person to order products and services online through texting, or to participate in surveys and contests through texting. Twitter, another social computing tool, enables individual users and organizations to send text messages that do not exceed 140 characters to a large group of followers. Some phone company plans and services also allow users to text from a Web site to a phone at no cost to the user.

Picture messaging from a phone has also become quite popular, with many apps and service plans allowing photos to be sent as e-mail, text, or IM attachments. "Sexting" is a form of messaging that involves sending and receiving sexually suggestive or explicit messages or photographs. Some, but not all, sexting cases involve dating relationships gone bad or cyberbullying in which inappropriate content gone viral was used to embarrass victims. Sexting by and among minors under 18 years of age is illegal and has led to criminal prosecution of dozens of juveniles who took pictures of themselves without clothes on. In August 2010, federal prosecutors and child safety advocates reported increases in cases that involve sexual extortion that comes about after teens post naked pictures of themselves online. In some of these "sextortion" cases, teens with nude or sexually suggestive pictures of themselves online are being contacted by pornographers who threaten to expose them to family and friends unless the child agrees to have more pictures or video of themselves taken in even more explicit poses or activities.[7] On June 6, 2011, Aurora Eller appeared on *The View* television show along with her parents and attorney Parry Aftab, who is the executive director of the nonprofit organization WiredSafety.[8] Eller explained how in 2008, when she was 13 years old, she took compromising photos of herself and posted them in a chat room, and was blackmailed by a cyberpredator if she did not send more. Now, at the age of 16, she is being charged with multiple counts of distributing child pornography.[9]

Danger also exists when a cell phone user texts or calls someone while they are driving. Most states now ban operating a cell phone while driving unless it can be done hands-free. In June 2007, five girls, all students of Fairport Central High School in Fairport, New York, died tragically in a horrific traffic accident just after graduation. Investigation revealed that a text message was sent from the driver's cell phone immediately prior to the impact of the girls' SUV with an oncoming truck, leading authorities to believe texting was a contributing factor.[10]

E-mail, or electronic mail, offers the ability to send and receive messages over an intranet, other telecom network, or the Internet. Everyone understands that e-mail can be viewed when it is received and also stored on a mail server often maintained by a company or other organization on behalf of employees. However, companies such as Google, Yahoo!, Hotmail, and Mail.com promote social computing by providing users with free e-mail accounts that allow varying storage capacities for messages and attachments. Unlike with texting or instant messaging, responses to e-mail may be delayed several hours, days, or even longer depending on several factors. By implication this form of social computing can be used to slow interactions down, which has advantages in certain situations. E-mail remains a tried, true, and preferred means of communication for business-related and official online correspondence and is critical to social computing of a professional nature.

Digital Internet Youth Culture

The emergence of the Internet and computing technology has spurred a new digital Internet culture in which many young people immerse themselves. In 2001, Marc Prensky referred to young people growing up now as "digital natives" because they had never known a world without the Internet. The term was contrasted with adults over age 24, who Prensky called "digital immigrants" because as a group they lived while the Internet was being created and becoming publicly used. Whereas digital natives naturally use IT devices and the Internet with which they have grown up, digital immigrants sometimes do not fully comprehend or even consider how technology can aid them in their daily tasks.[11]

Young people in computerized societies are increasingly using and surrounding themselves with IT devices and the Internet in their daily activities. They love their devices and social computing. They also like to solve problems in teams, be creative with technology, and discuss what is happening in the connected world. Social networking sites, chatting (online and texting), blogging, and electronic gaming are integral aspects of their life. Being online a lot and sending rapid-fire messages to friends and family are very important to them.

Young people often use *leetspeak* abbreviations such as LOL (laughing out loud) to speed up and sometimes disguise the meaning of communications in certain instances (e.g., POS = parent over shoulder). Leet (spelled online as L33T) came about when early computer programmers used only text on pre-Web bulletin board systems to communicate as efficiently as possible. Programmers who could express themselves with elegant programming and leet were considered elite by their peers—hence, elite speak and "leetspeak."

Digital youth culture bodes well for most young Internet users who, through social computing, come to know and interact with people like and also different from themselves. Overall their online interactions and experiences are positive. However, for some users social computing involves sending and/or receiving messages that are rude, insulting, or abusive, promiscuous or sexually charged in unwanted ways, or even criminal in nature. Many professionals throughout the world now believe that young people need to be educated and properly supervised to use IT devices and the Internet in ways that are safe, secure, and responsible. Young people themselves desire enjoyable social computing environments which minimize online hassles with other users. Terms of Use Agreements established by reputable social computing firms and Web sites reinforce these beliefs, though users of all ages seldom, if ever, read these online documents. With passage of new laws and implementation of education programs about Internet safety and online citizenship, digital natives and immigrants alike are becoming more aware and concerned about not becoming engaged in risky, criminal, or unethical behaviors online.

Internet Risks

Patty wears braces, and she is very pretty. She maintains appropriate photos of herself online and enjoys using Facebook. She has met many nice people online. She also interacts with her mom and 19-year-old sister on Facebook, which her mom requires as a condition of Patty keeping the account. Patty says this kind of rule is not true for most kids her age who go online with little if any parental supervision or interaction; certainly not for older kids, who she thinks are wiser for having learned plenty of lessons from each other about the need to be careful online.

Patty understands there are risks involved in being online, including loss of privacy that comes about after people share passwords or confidential information. She has already experienced friends giving out information she intended to remain private and some creepy things. She also knows that some people seem to become lost to their IT devices and Internet activities such as with excessive social computing and online gaming. For these reasons Patty controls who can view her Web page and as far as she knows, all the people she interacts with live in America. However, she quietly admits that it is possible—quite possible—that some of the people she interacts with online may not be who they claim to be.

In health class Patty learned about pedophiles, who are mostly adult men who try to have inappropriate sexual contact with girls and boys. So far she has not had any really bad experiences online. One time, however, she accepted a friend on Facebook who claimed he lived in a neighboring county. They became acquainted online, and he told Patty that he was old enough to drive and wanted to visit her at her house. That was when she became nervous, tried to stop communicating, and eventually removed him as a Facebook friend. It has now been several weeks and she has not heard anything more from this person, but she still worries that he is out there lurking in cyberspace.

The Internet allows people to interact with few constraints on their physical location, to do research, and to communicate with friends and family while on the go. Businesses have utilized this technology to improve services for customers and improve their overall sales presence online. Schools have used the Internet to teach students in new ways. In the process, schools promote safe and responsible use of the Internet. Even with these and many other positive things about the Internet, it still poses risks to users, including: losing personal data and loss of privacy, becoming victimized through online abuse or cybercrime, and losing perspective on oneself and real-world things. By understanding these risks users can better protect themselves to enjoy the Internet and Web content to its fullest.

RISKS OF LOSING CONFIDENTIAL DATA AND PERSONAL PRIVACY

Common risks associated with using the Internet include losing confidential data and loss of personal privacy. Individual users in many situations, whether they are an employee in a business office, a student in a class, a doctor in a hospital, or a person using a computer for online shopping, are all susceptible to losing confidential data. Once connected to the Internet, every user's system, device, or data may be compromised and even without their knowing it.

Part of the reason for this is that electronic messages sent over the Internet are transmitted and received in basically the same way as telegraph and early telephone systems, which also relied on electricity being sent over wires to convey messages that were susceptible to being intercepted. The main difference is that modern computers and software programs of today now route messages automatically without assistance of human telegraphers or telephone operators. However, just as with messages sent with earlier forms of technology, messages sent with modern IT devices may not remain private for two reasons.

First, anyone with access to data sent over a telecommunications network may be able to hear or read messages that are not sufficiently protected from prying ears or eyes with encryption. This is especially true for system administrators who are authorized to access and read data in order to monitor and maintain networks, and for hackers who may illegally access information systems connected to the Internet. Both system administrators and hackers are computer-savvy people who use software tools to manage IT devices and systems. Whereas system administrators are employed to protect the confidentiality, integrity, and availability of information, hackers act alone or in small groups to illegally access data for all sorts of reasons. Every day thousands of hackers discover ways to illegally access new sources of confidential data online. Once they have access to an information system, they may simply lurk to read unencrypted files and messages, or they may use existing software or write new code to copy, completely steal, destroy, change, delete, or deny access to portions of or all information contained within the system.

Today, online protection services and antivirus software are provided by companies like Norton and McAfee. These firms, among many others including Microsoft and other software developers, specialize in keeping up with and defeating known hacker exploits (i.e., system vulnerabilities). Professionals at these companies write code called *definitions,* which, once installed on a user's computer or other IT device, work to identify and defeat malware such as computer viruses, Trojan horses, worms, and spyware. Users of the Internet simply must use such services and products to keep their systems and data secure. Merely accessing the Internet for a few seconds with an unprotected device exposes it to attacks from all over cyberspace.

The second reason information sent online may not remain private is that people who receive messages may improperly share them with other people, perhaps by copying an original message into subsequent messages or by posting an original message online. Improper sharing of information frequently occurs because people are unaware of or insensitive to the intentions of the original sender to keep information confidential. A good rule of thumb to avoid problems of this kind is to simply not post anything that needs to remain private. Users need to realize that everything typed and saved or sent with an IT device (indeed, every key punch a person makes!) is potentially discoverable. Internet users must also realize that even if someone is texting or e-mailing another person located just across a street, the actual data containing the message may be transmitted in seconds throughout faraway parts of the Internet around the world before it arrives on the device for which it was intended. This provides many possible locations from which data can be intercepted.

Global messaging is made possible by sending data packets from and to IT devices with a unique Internet protocol (IP) address. Whenever a signal passes through a relay point, IP addresses are logged. IP addresses keep devices and therefore their owners from being truly anonymous. Just like all cars and trucks have a vehicle identification number (VIN) that is recorded and then assigned license plate registration numbers before they can be driven on highways, the IP address of computers and cell phones used on the Internet is effectively registered with ISP companies. Oftentimes it is the IP address of devices used in sending and receiving digital messages that enable law enforcement officers to identify and locate people suspected of committing cybercrimes.

The amount of privacy a user has and is entitled to depends at least on the country in which they live, the circumstances in which they are involved, the nature of the information in question, and their age, among many other factors. In general, children have less expectation of privacy and therefore fewer legal rights to privacy than adults; their privacy is usually granted to and overseen by parents or adult guardians. As people age and use more types of IT devices for more and varied things, reasonable expectations for what should and can remain private increase. In several historic cases, the United States Supreme Court has interpreted the U.S. Constitution as granting adults in the United States a right to privacy in their homes or private living areas and vehicles they own; of their body, clothing, and personal effects; and of their documents whether these are digitized or printed on paper.

Privacy also depends on whose device or system is being used. Teens, for example, may reasonably expect that their cell phone and its contents are private. However, parents who purchased the device or pay for its service plan are responsible for phone activities and therefore entitled to restrict or monitor phone usage by their children. Schools may also restrict use of IT devices and seize them if used improperly. Similarly, courts in the United States have ruled that adult employees who use company computers have no expectation of privacy. Many organizations prohibit employees from engaging in personal computing while using company equipment. Some organizations also monitor computer activity of its employees and will take disciplinary action when warranted.

Once information is voluntarily shared it can no longer be considered private. Posting anything online is like talking in front of people in public, even if the message is shared in private and intended to remain confidential. Online words no longer belong to only the person who sent or posted them. Anyone can share them, even against the wishes of a sender, and anyone who reads or listens to messages posted in public forums such as social networking forums is entitled to think about and respond to the words. So information posted to Web communities, blogs, chat rooms, and so forth is not private and also runs the risk of becoming viral if other users refer to it (perhaps with URL links) or copy it into content for further distribution online. The simple truth is that information posted online may not remain private even if users want it to.

A variety of digital technologies currently exist to help monitor and track individuals and systems. Within the medical field, for example, digital pacemaker technology is available to monitor and even help adjust a patient's heart rate. For years, electronic monitoring systems have also allowed the judicial system to monitor the whereabouts of suspected criminals or parolees. New software such as Google Latitude offers GPS tracking capabilities to individuals,

PRIVACY IN THE DIGITAL AGE

With computerization, the United States and many other countries have passed laws to help protect individual user's privacy. Many people believe, however, that maintaining personal privacy in the digital age is not possible. People who hold this view refer to the many ways in which data about people is collected and potentially used without their knowledge or permission. Financial data, medical and insurance records, education records, criminal records, and social services records typically all contain personal information of a private nature (e.g., a person's name, address, date of birth, Social Security number, etc.). It is the legal responsibility of government agencies and private firms to protect personal information once collected. However, rapid digital messaging and online crimes inherent to computerization make protecting any kind of data very difficult for organizations and users alike.

When someone swipes a bank card or uses a retail store membership card, purchasing information is recorded and sometimes

businesses, and government agencies that use computers or Web-enabled cell phones.

Geo-tagging refers to adding geographical information (i.e., longitude and latitude coordinates) as part of metadata of digital pictures, videos, Web sites, or text messages. Geo-tagging allows users to associate images with physical locations but cannot necessarily reveal the current location of the person. For this to occur, users need to use a service and software, such as provided by Foursquare, which enables smart phone users to *check in* online to identify their present location via Facebook, Twitter, or Web sites to anyone, including social-computing friends. Privacy

tracked. Stores and companies can then use this data to analyze consumer buying preferences and customize their advertising. Similarly, many other types of digital information is recorded by the government or private companies. This includes the Web sites people visit, the phone calls they make, and even the E-ZPass toll booths through which they travel.

Sometimes digital information collected about people is sold or used in ways they do not realize or understand, even though users often click that they have read, understood, and agreed with an organization's privacy policies, whether they have or not. Of course, information systems maintained by government and private sector organizations may be hacked, resulting in confidential data being stolen for use by cybercriminals. Under federal law and many state laws, users must be informed whenever a database containing private information is breached. In theory, people can then take steps to guard against becoming victimized through identity theft and other types of cybercrimes, but once personal data is stolen it is impossible to prevent it from being used by unauthorized people in all sorts of ways harmful to ordinary users.

concerns arise when smart phone users have not disabled the GPS locator software that may come pre-installed on their device. The fear is that physical locations of users can be tracked by ISPs, device or software manufacturers, or any other entity or person who could access geo-location data. In January 2011, Apple responded to concerns that iPhones, iPads, and iPods were automatically transmitting GPS location data of users whenever they engaged online. Company officials explained that the geo-location features of these devices were intended to enhance mapping and routing functions to aid but not spy on users; that geo-data recorded by these devices only identified cell towers and Wi-Fi hotspots near users' locations.[1] However, terms and conditions for using Apple's iTunes software (which backs up and synchronizes these devices with users' main computers) specifies that the company "collect, use and share precise location data including the real-time geographic location of your Apple computer or device." So even though location data is reportedly "collected anonymously in a form that does not personally identify users, it can be used by Apple, partnering firms, and licensees to provide and improve location-based products and services."[2] Controversy surrounding this issue resulted in two people filing a class action law suit against Apple over location-based services provided by its iOS 4 operating system software.

When people connect to the Internet and sign into various social networking Web sites, communication software, or online gaming sites, they invariably expose information about themselves beginning with the IP address of the device they are using. From that and through information on file with ISPs, a user's name, e-mail address, home address, phone number, age, and certain financial data can be learned. In addition, all information a user chooses to post online about themselves in social networking sites is subject to being collected and analyzed. In 2006, for example, a federal judge ruled that Google must comply with a subpoena to provide the U.S. Department of Justice with Web browsing history as part of a government effort ". . . to demonstrate the ease with which filtering

Canada's Privacy Commissioner, Jennifer Stoddart, speaks to the media about the changes to Facebook's privacy policy. The Canadian government pushed for changes to the social network after it was discovered that Facebook violated the country's Personal Information and Protection and Electronic Documents Act. *(Source: AP Photo/The Canadian Press, Adrian Wyld)*

software designed to keep minors from viewing pornography and other content online can be circumvented."[3]

Networking sites offer users the ability to share almost anything they feel comfortable sharing, including explicit content in some cases. By sharing this information with networking sites, communication software, gaming sites, and other Web sites, users give away personal information that could be used by companies, governments, employers, or others. Once personal data is posted—whether it is factual or not—friends, family, and strangers have the ability to read and further share that information. Social networking sites such as Facebook, MySpace, Twitter, and others offer privacy settings; however, one should understand that privacy settings are only effective if the potential information gatherer cannot find a way around them.

Digital youth culture promotes information sharing, engaging in teams to creatively solve technology-related problems, and a buddy system for peers to stay connected with each other.[4] Young users feel secure online based on the fact that friends and family are only an

PRIVACY CONCERNS WITH FACEBOOK

In 2007, it was revealed that Facebook users unwittingly exposed certain personal details about themselves on the site despite having set privacy settings to prevent unauthorized sharing of personal information. Privacy officers at Facebook were alerted to the problem by a blog post. "The situation meant that anyone could search for a user's name and, by narrowing the query according to various categories, find out details that the user did not intend to disclose."[5]

According to the same source, Facebook Chief Privacy Officer Chris Kelly stated that, "If [users] undertook an advanced search, it may have been possible to see a piece of information in a person's profile, even if that profile was private." Facebook administrators also acknowledged it had been a mistake not to have privacy settings available right along with specific kinds personal profile information.

It is now easier to understand and set privacy settings in Facebook in ways that will not reveal confidential information intended only for designated online friends. However, numerous Facebook users felt betrayed and regretted that their favorite social networking Web site company had not better guarded their confidential information in the first place.

instant message or text away. However, being constantly connected or expected to be available online can also lead to feelings of having one's privacy invaded. Merely by checking a user's social networking profile for a schedule or by viewing their online idle status, their location and activities may be learned. Out of respect for privacy and to remain safe online, the kinds and amount of information shared on the Internet with and about friends, family members, fellow students, and coworkers requires careful thought and constant attention.

RISKS OF BECOMING A VICTIM OF ONLINE ABUSE OR CYBERCRIME

A major study completed by researchers of the Rochester Institute of Technology (RIT) in 2007–2008 of more than 20,000 middle school and high school students revealed that young users of the Internet are at least as vulnerable to being abused or victimized online as adults. Among nearly 10,000 middle school students surveyed:[6]

- 21 percent reported they had experienced one or more forms of deceit or abuse within the previous (2006–2007) school year.
- Cyberbullying was common, with 15 percent reporting an embarrassing experience online and 13 percent indicating that they had been bullied or threatened online.
- 15 percent reported having another Internet user impersonate them online
- 11 percent reported that they had been asked to talk about sexual things online, and 14 percent admitted they had talked about sexual things online.
- 8 percent reported they had been exposed to nude pictures of other Internet users, and 7 percent reported that they were also asked for nude pictures of themselves online.

The RIT study also found that students were more likely to be victimized by people they actually know in person than by online strangers, and that a majority of known perpetrators were online friends or other young users rather than adults. Most students surveyed (53 percent) also admitted to committing many forms of online deceit, abuse, or crime. Lying about their age was the most common (24 percent). Nearly one in four (22 percent) reported they commonly downloaded music they did not pay for, and one in ten pretended to be someone else online. Bullying and sexually related abuses were less common among middle school students, with 4 percent admitting to intentionally embarrassing, harassing, or threatening another person online. Three percent of students admitted to asking for naked pictures from another Internet user, the same percent who sought to have sexual chat online.

Seven percent of middle school students reported they had gotten around security measures to access online content. Academic dishonesty committed by using computers or electronic devices to cheat on assignments and tests also occurred, with 5 percent of students admitting to online plagiarism, 5 percent admitting to cheating on school work, and 3 percent admitting to cheating on tests.

The findings of the RIT study revealed generally higher rates of victimization and offending experienced by and among high school students than middle school students. A major conclusion of this research is that people consistently begin to use the Internet with more kinds of IT devices earlier and earlier in life, and the possibilities for experiencing online deceit, abuse, or crime increase with amounts of time and varieties of online activities in which they engage. Simply stated, engaging in any amount of online activity exposes users to the possibility of becoming a victim. Fortunately there are many things users can do to avoid becoming harmed online.

RISKS OF LOSING ONESELF TO IT DEVICES AND WEB CONTENT

IT devices and the Internet are evolving and steadily encompassing many aspects of the home and educational, professional, travel, and public environments that people occupy on a daily basis. In the

PHONES ARE EASILY USED FOR CYBERBULLYING

Sarah dashes outside into the rain to catch the school bus. She accidentally drops her paper notebook *again* along the way, this time into a puddle. This happens often to Sarah, who is a bit clumsy and wears glasses with thick lenses. One student already on the bus opens a window and snaps a photo with the camera in his cell phone. The boy immediately uploads the photo onto a popular social computing Web site along with a comment. *"Hey look, four-eyes Sarah has done it again!"* Once onboard the bus, Sarah, only slightly wet and embarrassed, finds a seat among her friends who are now busy chatting with each other while also using their cell phones to talk or text with other friends and to browse the Internet. Sarah texts her best friend, "waz up?" She comments about being on the bus, gripes about her wet notebook, and posts how stupid she feels for having dropped it. Privately she fears what the boy in the back of the bus plans to do with the photo he snapped. She hopes the photo will not show up online. Too late. Her friend texts back that it had already been posted. Sarah is upset by the comments, which continue for several more days with more kids piling on.

process more people are using the Internet more often for more reasons and in more ways with different kinds of IT devices. Software applications for personal communications, entertainment, commerce, and research are now available for mobile computers and smart phones such as Blackberry, iPhone, and Droid devices. There are many benefits to this. One teen recently revealed in an interview for this book that her brother, who had always wanted to serve in the military, was deployed to Iraq in 2007 with his best friend. She and her parents were afraid he could be injured or killed in this war-torn

Jaron Lanier, a digital pioneer and Internet philosopher, believes that group thinking has discouraged individual opinions and innovation on the Web. *(Source: Kevin P. Casey/Bloomberg via Getty Images)*

nation. However, she also revealed that she was able to sleep every night and worry less because computer telephoning with Skype made it possible to speak with her brother often. Millions of people now rely on Skype when traveling or living abroad to communicate with friends throughout the world. Skype also makes video and conference calling very accessible and affordable.

As users continue to purchase broadband ISP connection services and expanded data plans to become even more involved in online computing activities, they are increasingly dependent on the Internet for many things in their lives. Despite all the virtues of living partially online and with the Internet, some users rely too much on IT devices or have blind faith in the reliability of Internet content.

Author and virtual pioneer Jaron Lanier is one of many Internet philosophers who have advocated for more individualized and humanistic aspects to being online. They worry that the Internet too often has the effect of aggregating users into groups, such as consumers of particular types of products and services, rather than respecting them for the individual people they actually are.[7] Other researchers, thinkers, and policy makers worry about individuals spending too much time online to risk becoming addicted to online activities such as texting, online gaming, or viewing sexual content. On the basis of major research conducted at the Rochester Institute of Technology,[8] author Sam McQuade concludes that the most active young online gamers (a relatively small percentage) are also prone to substance abuse and committing various forms of online abuse and crime. His research is generally consistent with

JUST FOR FUN—TRY BEING PRODUCTIVE WITHOUT USING IT DEVICES

Have you ever tried to write a school paper without a computer or cell phone? Many people feel a need to be connected to the Internet just to get ideas rather than relying on their personal knowledge or experiences. These people feel they "need" their IT devices and the Web to engage in imaginative or critical thinking. However, many students discover how much brain power *they* actually have and how too much information readily available online and how the mere process of trying to use IT devices can cloud their mind when they are disconnected from the Internet.

other major research findings that conclude that young people prone to experiencing problems off-line tend to have difficulty online as well.[9] Consequently all users of the Internet should think about why they go online and how much time they spend online in comparison to off-line activities, which are also important in the lives of healthy people. It is every individual's responsibility to take steps to protect personal data and privacy, avoid becoming abused or victimized online, and to maintain balanced use of IT devices.

Future Hopes
for Interacting Online

This year Mike, a senior in high school, is completing his last social studies class prior to graduation. The class is learning about politics and governance in other countries. This is interesting to Mike, who is considering going to college to pursue a career through which he can contribute to issues like human rights, social justice, and equality, or perhaps green environmental causes. He likes the class a lot because students use social computing to interact with and learn about students in other countries. Recently he has been following democratization movements in several countries in the Middle East. In the process he learned that Libya, even before its recent revolution, was very concerned about soil and water pollution from oil. He also learned that women in Saudi Arabia are not allowed to drive cars and must manage their personal and business financial affairs in banks separate from men.

During lunchtime Mike uses his laptop computer to conduct more research on social, political, and/or economic stability in

Middle East countries. He focuses on Egypt, which, in 2011, instituted a new government amid protest and social computing by citizens that captured the attention of media and people online throughout the world. He hopes to obtain native opinions, experiences, or other kinds of information from Egyptians with Internet access. So Mike signs onto Facebook and updates his status:

> **Mike Jones** *Is looking for a friend from Egypt to help with project information!*

He thought this would be a good way to obtain some fast, personal, indigenous information. Mike knows people in Egypt have Internet access, but is it filtered? He heard that in China the government filters Internet content to prevent Chinese people from accessing or disseminating certain kinds of content. He also heard that Syria and Iran blocked the free flow of information online to prevent political unrest. However, an exchange student Mike previously friended on Facebook had recently reposted his status in Cairo, Egypt. Maybe he would respond. Sure enough, only a day later, Hamadi K. checked in on Twitter as Hamadi003.

> **@Hamadi003** *Police lash out in plaza today! Avoid Market Street . . .*

Random thoughts bounce through Mike's head: What does that mean?! He is amazed that he is friends with someone in Cairo. Wow, are police in Cairo really out of control as indicated by Hamadi? Might Hamadi003 be at risk for expressing himself online? Will he get hurt? Mike sensed he could learn a lot from Hamadi's tweets about what was happening in Egypt. He marveled that someone his own age was talking to him about government transition in real time from half way around the world. Then another tweet:

> **@Hamadi003** *Sister harassed for the 5th time in streets today . . . Cairo Gov't we need peace please.*

Hamadi003 and Mike begin tweeting back and forth. In the process Mike gleans a lot of information for his project, but he also feels caught up in the real-life drama that Hamadi is experiencing. Then another link on Twitter and Mike's Facebook wall:

> **@Hamadi003** *www.cairotruth.ca.egy CLICK for the truth about our Gov't*

Mike clicks and suddenly his McAfee security software pops up and shows the following message:

> *WARNING: PUP Found. The file c:\\WINDOWS\CAIRO\ info.exe is a potentially Unwanted Program (Spyware, adware, or other malware) and has been blocked from running on your computer. If you do not recognize it, remove this PUP. If you recognize it, trust this PUP, and then rerun the program that triggered this ALERT.*

Mike is startled by what just happened. Previously when he received security warnings like this he learned that his laptop was vulnerable to damage if he did not immediately take steps to protect his system. Obviously the message apparently sent from Hamad003 intended to trick him into clicking on malware, which could corrupt his computer. Mike knows what to do next to protect his system, but he wonders whether Hamadi003, his "friend," intended to send a contaminated message. Who really is Hamadi003 and what are his intentions? What consideration or support did he owe to Hamadi?

Mike feels frustrated because only moments before he was gathering project information and enthralled by interacting with Hamadi, and now his technology might be compromised. Mike has reservations about re-contacting Hamadi as he begins to take technical steps to safeguard his device and data. He has the freedom and ability to obtain information from anywhere and anyone. Now he only wonders what was true and what exactly had led to him receiving the warning message. Also, what was the validity of his source and what was really happening in Cairo? Mike realizes that although he can friend anyone online, perhaps he cannot trust some people to convey legitimate information. As a netizen in the Information Age, he feels alone with his computer amid the vulnerabilities, limitless boundaries, and unknowns of cyberspace.

As the world embraces the Internet, people are educating themselves and each other about the exciting opportunities for interacting online. In the process more and more people continue to use the Internet for productive and enjoyable things, but also, unfortunately, for abusive and criminal purposes. Two goals are at once hopeful and challenging for future use of the Internet. One goal pertains to sound information being accessible to people as a means of promoting human rights, equality, and social justice along with commerce and transparency in government. This relates to hopes for *online literacy* and *democratization*, the idea that people have a right and responsibility to learn how to use IT devices and access information online to better their own lives and society regardless of socioeconomic and political circumstances. A second goal centers on preventing online abuse, cybercrime, and threats to critical information infrastructure because these things interfere with people using the Internet for productive and enjoyable purposes.

INFORMATION ACCESS, LITERACY, AND DEMOCRATIZATION

A prevailing philosophy practiced and understood by many users of the Internet centers on the belief that access to information and digital content should be as free and unrestricted as possible. For example, when going online, people have come to expect a browser app such as Google, Internet Explorer, or Bing to provide them with unfettered access to information they seek. Monetary costs associated with this often relate to commercial costs of developing software, manufacturing hardware, providing ISP accounts, installing and maintaining Internet infrastructure, and so on. However, the value of content actually provided online by search engines also depends at least on:

1. the amount and usefulness of online content posted by users or organizations (including hard-copy documents such as public records scanned into digital archives)
2. search terms used to locate particular kinds of content
3. how search engines are configured to prioritize content listed in response to searches
4. controls established by governments, organizations, or parents or guardians over what users of information systems are allowed to access
5. technological capabilities of IT devices used by people that seek information
6. a person's knowledge about how Web content is linked, combined with their technical ability to navigate online.

To the extent one or more of these things is compromised, information to be found online and the potential knowledge it may provide will be diminished. This means that just because seemingly infinite amounts of information can be found online, everything known or that could be shared online is not necessarily reliable. Further, many people, often through no fault of their own, are unable to access information they may be entitled to or need. Not being able to access the Internet may be due to technological infrastructure not reaching a geographic area, a person not owning or having access to an Internet-capable IT device, not knowing how to connect, or having insufficient funds to pay for Internet service along with being unable to access a public library. This implies that many people, including those who already use the Internet, are disadvantaged or may be discriminated against. This is cause for concern because throughout history, access to information has enabled people to flourish. It has often been said and written that information is power. Indeed, stable democracies and thriving markets depend on freedoms related to free-flowing information. Furthermore, being able to access and use information leads to new ideas in education and for technology innovations that bring about more efficient and effective products and services and can lead to higher rates of employment, better government, and other benefits.

The Internet is now paramount to maintaining the very nature of computerized, thriving, and free societies. Many nonprofit organizations, schools, commercial firms, and government agencies now directly or indirectly work to advance technology literacy and democratization. For example, the Center for Democracy and Technology (CDT) founded in 1994 and based in Washington, D.C., ". . . works to promote democratic values and Constitutional liberties in the digital age. As a civil liberties group with expertise in law, technology, and policy, CDT works to enhance free expression and privacy in communications technologies by finding practical and innovative solutions to public policy challenges while protecting civil liberties. CDT is dedicated to building consensus among all parties interested in the future of the Internet and other new communications media."[1] Similarly, "the Open Society Foundations (OSI), [founded by George Soros in 1984], work to build vibrant and tolerant democracies whose governments are accountable to their citizens. To achieve this mission, the Foundations seek to shape public policies that assure greater fairness in political, legal, and economic systems and safeguard fundamental rights. On a local level, the Open Society Foundations implement a range of initiatives to advance justice, education, public health, and independent media. At the same time, [they] build alliances across borders and continents on issues such as corruption and freedom of information. The Foundations place a high priority on protecting and improving the lives of people in marginalized communities."[2] These and many other nonprofit, commercial, and government organizations now collaborate online and in other ways to advance social justice and democratization by advocating for human rights, free sharing of information, privacy, security, and safety.

Many believe that the Internet should be free, without any restrictions or costs. Richard Stallman, a computer programmer and activist, is a free software advocate and refuses to use patented computer programs such as Microsoft Windows. *(Source: AP Photo/Aijaz Rahi)*

Seeking social justice is nothing new. Long before the Internet was invented and long after its development into a World Wide Web for linking content and users, people have organized to advance creation, posting, discovery, and sharing of information. However, the Internet and World Wide Web have transformed the nature of information as well as how it is created, shared, and stored. This underscores the importance of technology literacy. People need to have knowledge, skill, and ability to use IT devices and the Internet in responsible ways for productive and enjoyable purposes.

In recognition of this the Open Source Community has, for many years, included people from all over the world who believe in sharing information online through development of *freeware*, or free software. Freeware was first conceived of by Richard Stallman who founded the Open Source Initiative in 1998. This nonprofit

WHITE HAT AND BLACK HAT HACKERS

Not all hackers engage in illegal activities. In fact the original hackers were model railroaders who were also electrical engineering students at the Massachusetts Institute of Technology (MIT). Beginning in the late 1950s, they used early computer technology and programming code to solve problems. Intense curiosity coupled with technical skills drove them to acquire access to computer systems and computerized information controlled by their university. These efforts eventually lead to creation of the hacker ethic and a subculture of secretive and very skilled computer users.[3] By the late 1970s, as computer systems came to be more relied on throughout society, computer hacking was steadily criminalized by states and countries that enacted computer crime laws.[4]

From this history emerged a somewhat vague and argumentative distinction between White Hat and Black Hat hackers. White Hats use their hacking skills "for good," typically to discover and even fix security vulnerabilities in computer operating systems and software applications. Competent system administrators possess legitimate hacking abilities—this is what makes them good at their jobs. Black Hat hackers are just the opposite. They use their technical knowledge and skills to illegally access information systems and data. Their goals include stealing or destroying data such as passwords or confidential employment, medical, or education information. Use of Black Hat hackers by corporations to spy (e.g., on other firms) is illegal and employing hackers in service of governments to carry out cyberespionage or information warfare is controversial.

Richard Stallman has epitomized what White Hat hackers do. In 1983, he founded the GNU Project, dedicated to creating soft-

organization "consists of an evolving group of individuals and organizations interested in collaborating on the development of the best nonproprietary, open source electronic portfolio code possible . . .

ware and making it free for people to use. He began to hack when he was a college student attending the Massachusetts Institute of Technology (MIT). His exploits included unauthorized modifying of password and printer codes to overcome restricted access and other inconveniences experienced by system users. In the process he became "convinced . . . of the ethical need to require free software" and is widely recognized for conceiving of freeware and founding the Open Source Initiative in 1998.[5] Working with organizations such as the Free Software Foundation and League for Programming Freedom, he continues to promote free software and free access to software. Stallman has received wide recognition for his commitment to Open Source Community principles and has received four honorary doctoral degrees. He has never been charged with or prosecuted for violating computer crime laws.

By comparison, Black Hat hacker Jonathan James became famous as the first juvenile to serve time in a federal prison in connection with having hacked into a server of the U.S. Defense Threat Reduction Agency (DTRA). James secretly installed a backdoor on the system, giving him unauthorized access to digital records of this agency which guards against threats from nuclear, biological, chemical, conventional, and special weapons. He also hacked into NASA computers and stole software (valued at $1.7 million) used to support environmental conditions for astronauts living on the International Space Station. Known by his nickname "c0mrade," James, who was only 16 years old at the time of his crimes, was sentenced to six months incarceration, placed under house arrest, and banned from recreational computing. After violating terms of his probation, he served the remainder of his sentence in prison.[6]

OSI is actively involved in Open Source community-building, education, and public advocacy to promote awareness and the importance of nonproprietary software."[7] As such OSI bridges commercial computing sectors with noncriminal aspects of the hacker subculture and what is now regarded as *ethical hacking*.[8] Many colleges and universities that sponsor programs of study in computer science, software engineering, IT, or systems administration teach students how to use ethical hacking methods to diagnose and fix problems that occur on information systems and networks. Professional development training firms such as the Computer Security Institute (CSI), SANS, and InfoSec Institute also provide beginning, advanced, and technical courses for adults employed as system administrators, information security professionals, or computer forensic examiners.

TWITTER JOINS FACEBOOK AND GOOGLE AS SOCIAL COMPUTING MEDIUM

Public officials, celebrities, and ordinary people now use the Internet in various ways to communicate and get things done. However, Twitter, which currently allows users to "tweet" messages up to 140 characters long, is the very latest and popular means of interacting online for personal and professional purposes. Millions of people use Twitter to update their daily activities and thoughts about things to other types of social computing outlets such as their Facebook profiles. Organizations also invite people to tweet questions, comments, and links to things of interest. Twitter is now being used by powerful mainstream institutions.

On June 29, 2011, the Pope tweeted for the first time and the Vatican's English-language Twitter feed now has more than 50,000

The Internet enables unprecedented information sharing. Official and self-organizing virtual efforts to promote information sharing, practice technology literacy, and implement democracy are now playing out in exciting ways. Social computing is an especially important online means for accomplishing these things. In addition to providing billions of people with forums through which they can share and learn, multimedia social computing is contributing in many ways to movements and major changes now occurring throughout the world. Throughout 2011, social computing factored into overthrowing and transitioning of governments in the Middle East. Increasingly e-mail, blogs, group forums, Facebook, and Twitter, among many other online outlets and resources, are empowering individuals as well as organizations to affect world events with online content.

followers. Previously the Vatican ". . . joined Facebook and YouTube in an effort to connect with younger, digitally savvy generations . . . Social-media outreach programs [of the Catholic Church] are grouped on the Pope 2 You site, run by the Pontifical Council for Social Communications."[9] Only days later, on July 6, 2011, Twitter hosted "Town Hall at the Whitehouse," which featured U.S. President Barack Obama tweeting some responses to thousands of people who tweeted @AskObama to ask questions about all kinds of policy issues.[10]

Colleges, universities, media outlets, and other kinds of companies are also going online to establish Twitter as well as Facebook and Google accounts to leverage their social computing outreach and for things like cloud computing that enables users to store applications and documents in cyberspace rather than on computer servers or hard drives. It seems that everyone conceives of and uses the Internet differently. In effect the Internet is as unique as its users and the Web content that they contribute. All of this bodes well for future use of the Internet, but only to the extent that the Internet and information systems are safe to use.

PREVENTING CYBER ABUSE AND CYBERCRIME

Every day, as people throughout the world enjoy living with the Internet, online abuse, cybercrime, and threats to critical information infrastructure occur and in small to large ways interfere with how the Internet helps society. Online abuse involves activities like using IT devices to plagiarize, cyberbully, or intentionally violate computer account policies. Sometimes online abuse can become a cybercrime, as in violations of intellectual property or copyright laws (e.g., pirating), threatening someone, or exceeding computer account permissions to trespass into an unauthorized area online. More serious threats against information systems, such as those used to control electrical power or national security, also involve cybercrimes. In the digital age the most serious instances of such attacks may constitute acts of terrorism or even war. Living safely, securely, and responsibly with the Internet is serious business.

Fortunately many things are being done to improve Internet safety and security. Software apps and IT devices now usually come equipped with privacy and security features that allow users to adjust configuration settings. Users are learning how to reset default settings, filter or block unwanted messages, and generally protect themselves along with their devices and data from all sorts of online attacks. Schools are increasingly teaching students about these topics. Parents and guardians are also learning about online abuse by and among young Internet users while also becoming more accepting and supportive of digital youth culture. Employers are improving Internet-related security and safety practices within their organizations. Many organizations have instituted acceptable use policies (AUPs) similar to those now being created or adopted by schools to govern how the Internet and IT devices like cell phones are used. Through these efforts cyber-related abuse, crimes, and tragedies can be prevented.

On September 12, 2008, a Metrolink passenger train collided head-on with Union Pacific freight train near Los Angeles, California. Twenty-five people were killed and 135 others were injured in "one of the deadliest rail accidents in California history."[11]

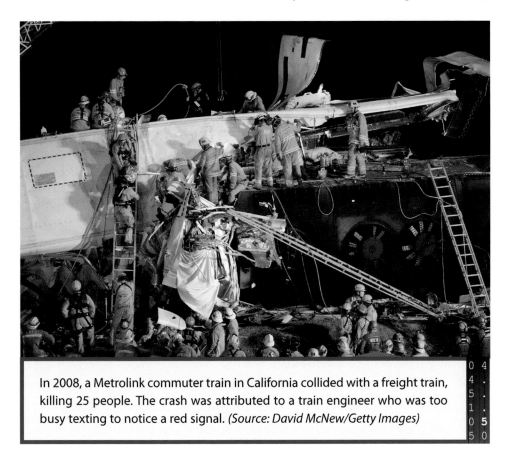

In 2008, a Metrolink commuter train in California collided with a freight train, killing 25 people. The crash was attributed to a train engineer who was too busy texting to notice a red signal. *(Source: David McNew/Getty Images)*

Federal investigators determined that the Metrolink train engineer was sending text messages at the time of the collision, which evidently caused him to run through a red train signal. As the result of this and other railroad accidents involving employees being distracted while using cell phones, train companies throughout the country now restrict circumstances in which such devices can be used.[12] Similarly, traffic collisions on highways have led many states to ban using handheld IT devices while driving.

Many state and national laws now prohibit or require certain things to aid in preventing all sorts of cybercrimes. Less common are international agreements or treaties signed by countries committed to preventing cybercrimes or coordinating their efforts to investigate and prosecute cybercrimes that often occur in transnational ways.

In 2006, the U.S. Senate, along with 38 other nations, ratified the Council of Europe Treaty on Cybercrime.[13] This treaty obligates all countries that signed the treaty to cooperate in international investigations and prosecutions of cybercriminals. Officers employed by local, state, and national government law enforcement agencies now investigate traditional crimes with an eye toward the ways in which IT devices and the Internet were involved. This is in addition to dedicated cybercrime investigators and computer forensic analysts who specialize in investigating technical ways in which people suspected of committing crimes online used their IT devices and the Internet. Common types of cyberabuse and cybercrime now include: hacking, distributing malware, intellectual property (IP) theft, piracy, making online threats, credit card or bank fraud, illicit purchasing of prescription or illegal drugs, and various kinds of Internet sex crimes including those that involve minors (e.g., creating, possessing, or distributing child pornography) and human trafficking (e.g., for purposes of prostitution).

Information security professionals are now employed by many types of companies, and also by government agencies and nonprofit organizations. These professionals help to prevent and investigate online abuses and cybercrimes committed by employees or other users of information systems. System administrators who maintain computers, intranets, and other types of networks that connect to the Internet also understand ways in which online abuse and crimes occur. They, too, work to prevent these things from happening in various types of organizations. Information security professionals and systems administrators usually acquire college education and also keep up their knowledge and skills through professional development training. Many professionals hold security credentials such as the Certified Information Systems Security Professional (CISSP) certification governed by the International Information Systems Security Certification Consortium, Inc. (commonly known as "ISC squared"). Possessing this or another credential certifies that an individual possesses certain knowledge and technical skills necessary to help secure computerized systems and devices.

Many resources are now available to help users learn about cybersecurity and safety. These include books, magazines, and social computing forums dedicated to information security. Educational

MINIMUM THINGS USERS SHOULD DO TO PROTECT THEIR NETWORKS, IT DEVICES, AND DATA

1. Use strong passwords consisting of at least 10 random alphanumeric characters that do not spell a name or word.
2. Keep passwords confidential, change them often and keep track of multiple passwords in a safe place such as on a slip of paper stuck into a book on a bookshelf filled with other books.
3. Use and update malware protection software often by subscribing to services offered by firms such as Norton Antivirus or McAfee Antivirus and/or reliable open source antivirus such as Spybot.
4. Install and use a software or hardware firewall, and never connect a device to the Internet until you do.
5. Update operating system and software applications frequently.
6. Backup data often, systematically, and in different ways.
7. Even if you are technically savvy, do not work from an account with root or administrator privileges so as to not accidentally lose or corrupt original system applications, files or data.
8. Learn more about and adopt information security practices into your lifestyle.

resources designed for students, teachers, and parents such as i-SAFE and NetSmartz also exist online at no cost. Hundreds of organizations also provide tips for how to be safe, secure, and ethical online. Among the very best provided by the U.S. government is OnGuard Online, which can be found at http://www.onguardonline .gov/. This Web site "provides practical tips from the federal government and the technology industry to help you be on guard against Internet fraud, secure your computer, and protect your personal information."[14]

● ● ● CHRONOLOGY ● ● ●

1600   England physician William Gilbert writes about his experiments with magnetism and "electrica."

1725   Punched cards are first used by Basile Bouchon and Jean-Baptiste Falcon to provide a machine with instructions (the earliest form of programming).

1752   Benjamin Franklin's theory that electricity and lightning are one in the same thing is proven.

1790   Optical telegraph semaphore stations are constructed throughout portions of Europe.

1830   American Joseph Henry discovers electricity can be used to send an electrical charge down a mile-long wire to ring a bell attached to an electromagnet (the basis for electric telegraph messages).

1835   Samuel Morse creates the famous Morse code used in telegraph messages.

1876   Alexander Graham Bell makes the first telephone call.

1879   Thomas Edison invents the light bulb.

1901   Transatlantic ship-to-shore and ship-to-ship radio telegraphy is first used.

1906   AM (amplitude modulation) radio is used to broadcast voice and music over airwaves.

1923   Radio facsimile (fax) machine is used to send a photograph wirelessly.

1929   Television technology allows people to hear and see a transmitted message.

1936   The Theory of Computing is devised by British mathematician Alan Turing.

1944   The Harvard Mark I Computer is created.

1946   AT&T creates the first public cellular phone service, and IBM creates the Electronic Numerical Integrator and Computer (ENIAC).

1957   IBM releases the first programming language, FORTRAN, used in its 650 Model Computer (the world's first mass-produced computer).

1958   Bell Telephone creates a modem that allows binary data to be sent over telephone lines.

1958   The first case of "computer abuse" is reported by a Minneapolis bank in an account fraud (which occurs prior to the creation of state or federal computer crime laws).

1958   The U.S. government's Advanced Research Projects Agency (ARPA) funds universities and laboratories to conduct research on computers.

1964   IBM introduces the word processor.

1969   The first commercial use of an Automatic Teller Machine (ATM) takes place with bank cards that contain personal security codes.

1971   E-mail is first sent and received over ARPANET, the forerunner network of the Internet.

1975   Microsoft Corporation is founded by William "Bill" Henry Gates III and Paul Allen.

1976   Apple Computer Inc. is founded by Steve Jobs and Ron Wayne.

1978   Cellular phones for commercial use are introduced.

1979   Electrical engineering students at Massachusetts Institute of Technology (MIT) tinker with model train layout switching from which the computer hacker subculture emerges.

1982   William Gibson coins the term *cyberspace*.

1983   More than 100 companies make personal computers. Approximately 5 million desktop computers are estimated to exist in United States alone, and about 3 million computer terminals are now "networked" with larger "host" computers.

1984   The public begins to use the Internet, and the U.S. Congress enacts the Computer Fraud and Abuse Act, which makes hacking into a government-controlled computer illegal.

1988   Robert T. Morris Jr. releases the first computer worm onto the Internet, marking the onset of "malware" (i.e., malicious computer code like worms, viruses, Trojans, and spyware). The self-replicating program crashes between 10 to 20 percent of the 60,000 to 80,000 computers then connected to the Internet.

1989   MP3 is invented and later becomes the most common format for music on the Internet.

1990   Schools begin to use personal computers (PCs).

1992   Delphi becomes the first Internet Service Provider.

1993   The Internet is commercialized, becomes widely known as the World Wide Web, and Microsoft releases Windows NT and Mosaic Web browser tools.

1994   Bluetooth Wireless Standard simplifies "frequency hopping" data communications between mobile devices.

1997   The term *weblog* is coined by Jorn Barger; Secure Electronic Transaction Initiative allows secure credit card transactions over the Internet.

1999   Shawn Fanning and Sean Parker create Napster, which allows people to share music files.

2000   I LOVE YOU (Love Bug) worm is released in more than 50 variations that strike 40 million computers all over the world, costing consumers and organizations $8.7 billion.

A&M Records and several other recording companies sue Napster for copyright infringement

2001   The Council of Europe treaty on cybercrime standardizes Internet crimes internationally.

Schools begin to use software to detect plagiarism by students (copying works of other people without giving them credit for their ideas).

Wikipedia becomes one of the most visited sites on the Web, and demonstrates possibilities for "wisdom of crowds" and "Web 2.0" applications.

2003   The Recording Industry Association of America (RIAA) begins to sue thousands of individuals for distributing copyrighted music files over peer-to-peer networks.

MySpace is created.

2004   Facebook is founded by Mark Zuckerberg, a student of Harvard University. The new social computing Web site was initially limited to college students attending Harvard. By 2006, anyone older than 13 years of age can join.

Gmail (e-mail from Google) begins to offer users 1 gigabyte of storage space for free.

2005   YouTube is created and becomes a major hub for social computing.

2006   Google Inc. purchases YouTube Corporation for $1.65 billion in Google stock.

Megan Meier commits suicide after experiencing a cruel online hoax. She is the first death victim of cyberbullying.

2007   A survey of 40,000 kindergarten through 12th-grade students reveals online abuse and Internet crime begins when children are as young as four years of age.

32 Australian teenagers are prosecuted for "sexting" (i.e., sending nude photos of themselves using a computer or cell phone).

2009 Online shopping grows more popular: Post-Thanksgiving "Cyber Monday" sales of merchandise are 30 percent higher than "Black Friday" store sales.

2010 More than 2 billion people use computers connected to the Internet.

ENDNOTES

INTRODUCTION

1. Infographic, "Change in Internet Access by Age Group, 2000–2009," Pew Internet & American Life Project, http://www.pew internet.org/Infographics/2010/Internet-acess-by-age-group-over-time.aspx (Accessed April 19, 2010).

2. Lee Rainie, "Internet, Broadband, and Cell Phone Statistics," Pew Internet & American Life Project, http://www.pewinternet.org/Reports/2010/Internet-broadband-and-cell-phone-statistics.aspx (Accessed April 19, 2010).

3. Infographic, "Portrait of a Twitter User: Status Update Demographics," Pew Internet & American Life Project, http://www.pewinternet.org/Infographics/Twitter-demographics--Fall-2009.aspx (Accessed April 19, 2010).

4. ——, "Adults on Social Network Sites, 2005–2009," Pew Internet & American Life Project, http://www.pewinternet.org/Infographics/Growth-in-Adult-SNS-Use-20052009.aspx (Accessed April 19, 2010).

CHAPTER 1

1. Frederick E. Allen, "Technology at the End of the Century: A Look at Where We've Been and Where We May Be Going," *Invention & Technology* (2000): 10–16.

2. Amy Friedlander, *Natural Monopoly and Universal Service: Telephones and Telegraphs in the U.S. Communications Infrastructure 1837–1940.* (Reston, Va.: Corporation for National Research Initiatives, 1995).

3. Amy Friedlander, *Emerging infrastructure: The Growth of Railroads.* (Reston, Va.: Corporation for National Research Initiatives, 1995).

4. Richard C. Dorf, *"Computers and Man,"* (San Francisco, Calif.: Boyd & Fraser Publishing Company, 1974), 9–25.

5. Andrew Hodges, "The Alan Turing Home Page," http://www.turing.org.uk/turing/scrapbook/ww2.html (Accessed September 19, 2011).

6. Scott Griffin, "Internet Pioneers," http://www.ibiblio.org/pioneers/bush.html (Accessed September 19, 2011).

7. Internet World Stats, "Internet Usage Statistics: The Internet Big Picture," http://www.internetworldstats.com/stats.htm (Accessed September 6, 2010).

CHAPTER 2

1. Staff Author, "Computer Languages Timeline," Levenez.com, 2010, http://www.levenez.com/lang/lang_a4.pdf (Accessed April 26, 2010).

2. James H. Evans, "21st-Century Software Development: Crowdsourcing Is the Future of Cell Phone Application Development," suite101.com, March 29, 2008, http://james-hvw-evans.suite101.com/android-us-

iphone-a47331 (Accessed April 26, 2010).

3. KeePass Password Safe, "Official Homepage of KeePass, the Free, Open-Source, Light-Weight and Easy to Use Password Manager," http://keepass.sourceforge.net/index.php (Accessed April 26, 2010).

4. Discovery Channel, "The American Power Outage of 2003," (New York, N.Y.: NBC News Productions, 2003).

CHAPTER 3

1. Texas Independent School District Austin, "Teacher Tools—Technology Equipment–Standard Classroom Setup," http://www.austinschools.org/techinfo/teach_tools/tech_equip/classr_setup.html (Accessed July 10, 2011).

2. Jonathan Guryan, "The Impact of Internet Subsidies in Public Schools," University of Chicago, http://faculty.chicagobooth.edu/austan.goolsbee/research/erate.pdf (Accessed July 10, 2011).

3. Staff Author, "PET 2001," Obsolete Technology, 2011, http://oldcomputers.net/pet2001.html (Accessed July 10, 2011).

4. C. J. Carr and Everett Q. Carr, "Teachers, Computers and the Classroom," *Compute!* 1 (Fall 1979): 42.

5. Margaret Kane, "eBay Picks Up PayPal for $1.5 Billion," Cnet News, http://news.cnet.com/2100-1017-941964.html (Accessed July 10, 2011).

6. CBS News, "Facebook, PayPal Users Urged to Check Logins After Hacking," http://www.cbc.ca/news/canada/prince-edward-island/story/2011/06/17/pei-lulzsec-personal-internet-accounts-584.html (Accessed July 10, 2011).

7. Brock Read, "Piracy and Copyright: An Ethics Lesson," http://chronicle.com/temp/email2.php?id=cnnGQrssdRzSvpjCtFpjv9n8JNqbZSm2 (Accessed May 19, 2005).

8. Science Applications International Corporation (SAIC), *Information Warfare: Legal Regulatory, Policy, and Organizational Considerations for Assurance,* (Washington, D.C.: Joint Staff, The Pentagon, 1995).

9. John D. McKinnon, "Estonia Presses Bush for Cyber-Attack Research Center," http://blogs.wsj.com/washwire/2007/06/25/estonia-presses-bush-for-cyber-attack-research-center/ (Accessed April 28, 2008).

10. John Lasker, "U.S. Military's Elite Hacker Crew." *Wired,* http://www.wired.com/news/privacy/0,1848,67223,00.html?tw=rss.TOP. (Accessed April 19, 2005).

11. Julian E. Siobhan and Barnes Gorman, "Cyber Combat: Act of War," Dow Jones & Company, Inc., http://online.wsj.com/article/SB10001424052702304563104576355623135782718.html?mod=WSJ_Tech_RightMostPopular#printMode (Accessed May 31, 2011).

CHAPTER 4

1. EducationWorld, National Standards, EducationWorld, http://www.educationworld.com/

standards/ (Accessed July 10, 2011).

2. Mike Frassinelli, "Facing Job Losses, Toll Collectors Demand N.J. Turnpike Authority Negotiate With Them," New Jersey .com, http://www.nj.com/news/index.ssf/2011/03/facing_job_losses_toll_collect/1607/comments.html (Accessed July 10, 2011).

3. Staff Author, "Find the Best Fit: We Pick Phones and Plans to Suit Varying Needs," *Consumer Reports.* (January 2011): 30–37.

4. Tomi T. Ahonen, "Thought Piece: Mobile Telecoms Industry Size 2009," Tomi Ahonen.com, http://www .abdn.ac.uk/~csc228/teaching/CS5011/information/abdn .only/TomiAhonenThoughts-MobileIndustrySize2009.pdf (Accessed July 11, 2011).

CHAPTER 5

1. Staff Author, "Facebook Statistics," http://www.facebook.com/press/info.php?statistics (Accessed September 11, 2011).

2. Jon Lockton, "The Social Impact of Facebook in 2011," The Hals Report, http://www.thehals report.com/2011/01/the-social-impact-of-facebook-in-2011/ (Accessed July 11, 2011).

3. Technortai Media, "About Technorati," 2009, http://technoratimedia.com/technorati_media/about.html (Accessed September 10, 2010).

4. Reuters, "Video Game Sales Overtaking Music," 2007, http://articles.moneycentral .msn.com/Investing/Extra/VideoGameSalesOvertaking Music.aspx. (Accessed June 26, 2007).

5. Staff Author, "Supreme Court Overturns California Gaming Law," PBNation, 2011, http://www.pbnation.com/showthread.php?t=3632797 (Accessed July 11, 2011).

6. IGN Blog Authors, "Games Industry Reacts to Supreme Court Decision: Publishers and Developers Thrilled with Ruling," IGN Enterprises, http://games.ign.com/articles/117/1179211p1.html (Accessed July 11, 2011).

7. Associated Press, "Feds: Online 'Sextortion' of Teenagers Is on the Rise: Texted Photos, Webcam Images Used by Blackmailers in Threats," *Democrat and Chronicle*, August 14, 2010, 22A.

8. Staff Author, "The *View* Show Summary Description," The View, June 6, 2011, http://theview.abc.go.com/recap/monday-june-6-2011 (Accessed July 11, 2011).

9. Erin Gallagher, "Sextortion: Online Predators are Using Technology and Peer Pressure to Blackmail our Kids," Channahon-Minooka Patch, http://channahonminooka.patch .com/articles/sextortion-mom-talk (Accessed July 11, 2011).

10. Ben Dobbin, "Texting While Driving? Message Sent from Driver's Phone: Records Show Text Message Exchange Around Time of Fatal Crash," (New York, ABC News, 2007).

11. Marc Prensky, "Digital Natives, Digital Immigrants," *On the Horizon* 9, no. 5 (October 2001): 1–6.

CHAPTER 6

1. Ki Mae Heussner, "Apple Responds to iPhone Tracking Controversy," World News with Diane Sawyer, ABC News .com. http://abcnews.go.com/ Technology/apple-responds-iphone-tracking-controversy/ story?id=13468295 (Accessed January 11, 2011).

2. Charles Arthur, "iPhone Keeps Record of Everywhere You Go: Privacy Fears Raised as Researchers Reveal File on iPhone that Stores Location Coordinates and Timestamps of Owner's Movements," *The Guardian*. http://www.guardian .co.uk/technology/2011/apr/20/ iphone-tracking-prompts-privacy-fears (Accessed July 12, 2011).

3. Eric Bangeman, "Google Will Have to Turn over Search Data to the Government," ars technica. http://arstechnica.com/ old/content/2006/03/6381.ars (Accessed July 12, 2011).

4. Samuel C. McQuade, James P. Colt and Nancy B.B. Meyer, *Cyber Bullying: Protecting Kids and Adults From Online Bullies*, (Westport, Conn.: Praeger, 2009), 12-20.

5. Jonathan Richards, "Facebook Admits Privacy Flaw: The Social Network has Acknowledged that Users May Unwillingly Have Been Exposing Details such as Sexual Preference They Meant to Keep Private," *Times* (London). http://technology .timesonline.co.uk/tol/news/ tech_and_web/article2005618 .ece (Accessed December 21, 2010).

6. Samuel C. McQuade and Neel Sampat, *RIT Survey of Internet and At-Risk Behaviors*, (Rochester, N.Y.: Rochester Institute of Technology, 2008).

7. Jaron Lanier, *You Are Not a Gadget*, (New York: Knopf, Borzoi Books—Random House, 2010).

8. McQuade and Sampat, 2008.

9. Berkman Center for Internet and Society, *Final Report of the Internet Safety Technical Task Force to the Multi-State Working Group on Social Networking of State Attorneys General of the United States*, (Cambridge, Mass.: Harvard Law School, 2008).

CHAPTER 7

1. Center for Democracy and Technology, "Keeping the Internet Open, Innovative and Free," CDT.org. http://www.cdt.org/ (Accessed July 14, 2011).

2. Open Society Foundations, "Home Page Mission Statement," Open Society Foundations, http://www.soros.org/ about (Accessed July 14, 2011).

3. Steven Levy, *Hackers: Heroes of the Computer Revolution*, (New York: Doubleday, 1984).

4. Donn B. Parker, *Computer Crime: Criminal Justice Resource Manual* (2nd ed). (Washington, D.C.: National Institute of Justice, 1989).

5. IT Security Editors, "Top 10 Most Famous Hackers of All Time," FOCUS, 2011, http://www

.focus.com/fyi/top-10-most-famous-hackers-all-time/ (Accessed July 13, 2011).

6. Ibid.

7. Open Source Initiative, "Web Home Page," http://www.opensource.org/ (Accessed July 14, 2011).

8. Samuel C. McQuade, *Understanding and Managing Cybercrime*, (Boston: Pearson Education, 2006), 236–238.

9. Greg Wilson, "The Pope Tweets for First Time," NBC Washington, http://www.nbcwashington.com/news/tech/The-Pope-Tweets-fo-First-Time-124661154.html (Accessed July 14, 2011).

10. Twitter, "Twitter Presents Townhall @ the White House," Twitter, http://askobama.twitter.com/ (Accessed July 15, 2011).

11. L.A. Now Staff Author, "Metrolink Engineers Probably Caused 2008 Rialto Train Crash, NTSB says," *Los Angeles Times*, April 28, 2011. http://latimesblogs.latimes.com/lanow/2011/04/metrolink-engineers-rialto-train-crash.html (Accessed July 15, 2011).

12. Andy Cummings, "Railroads: The Post-Cell Phone Era," *Trains*. (August 2011): 6–7.

13. Declan McCullagh and Anne Broache, "Senate Ratifies Cybercrime Treaty," CNET News, http://news.cnet.com/2100-7348_3-6102354.html (Accessed August 7, 2006).

14. Federal Trade Commission, "OnGuard Online," Federal Trade Commission. http://www.onguardonline.gov/ (Accessed December 21, 2010).

● ● ● BIBLIOGRAPHY ● ● ●

Bakardjieva, Maria. *Internet Society: The Internet in Everyday Life*. London: SAGE Publications, 2005.

Blair, Steven, Andrea L. Dunn, Bess H. Marcus, and Ruth Ann Carpenter. *Active Living Every Day*, 2d ed. Champaign, Illinois: Human Kinetics, 2010.

Carr, Nicholas. *The Shallows: What the Internet Is Doing to Our Brains*. London: W. W. Norton & Company Ltd., Castle House, 2011.

Castells, Manuel. *The Internet Galaxy: Reflections on the Internet, Business, and Society*. New York: Oxford University Press, 2003.

Comer, Douglas E. *The Internet Book: Everything You Need to Know about Computer Networking and How the Internet Works*. Upper Saddle River, NJ: Pearson Prentice Hall, 2007.

Creeber, Glen and Royston Martin. *Digital Culture: Understanding New Media*. New York: Open University Press, 2008.

Gralla, Preston. *How the Internet Works*, 8th ed. Indianapolis: Que Publishing/Pearson Education, 2006.

Gralla, Preston. *How Wireless Works*. Que Publishing/Pearson Education: Indianapolis, 2006.

Hobbs, Renee. *Digital and Media Literacy: Connecting Culture and Classroom*. Thousand Oaks, Calif.: Corwin/SAGE, 2011.

Howard, Phillip E. and Steve Jones. *Society Online: The Internet in Context*. Thousand Oaks, Calif.: SAGE Publications, 2004.

Gere, Charlie. *Digital Culture*. London: Reaktion Books, 2009.

Goldsmith, Jack and Tim Wu. *Who Controls the Internet? Illusions of a Borderless World*. New York: Oxford University Press, 2008.

McQuade, Samuel C. *Understanding and Managing Cybercrime*. Boston: Pearson/Allyn and Bacon, 2006.

Morozov, Evgeny. *The Net Delusion: The Dark Side of Internet Freedom.* Philadelphia: PublicAffairs Books/Perseus Books Group, 2011.

Moschovitis, Christos J. P. *History of the Internet.* Santa Barbara, Calif.: ABC-CLIO, 1999.

Mossberger, Karen, Caroline J. Tolbert and Ramona S. McNeal. *Digital Citizenship: The Internet, Society, and Participation.* Cambridge: Massachusetts Institute of Technology, 2007.

Okin, J. R. *The Internet Revolution: The Not-for-dummies Guide to the Impact, Perils, and Promise of the Internet.* White Harbor, Me.: Ironbound Press, 2005.

Ryan, Johnny. *A History of the Internet and the Digital Future.* London: Reaktion Books, 2010.

Sandler, Corey. *Living With the Internet and Online Dangers.* Plain City, Ohio: Library Journals LLC/Media Souce, Inc., 2010.

Schell, Bernadette H. *The Internet and Society: A Reference Handbook* (Contemporary World Issues). Santa Barbara, Calif.: ABC-CLIO, 2006.

Segaller, Stephen. *Nerds 2.0.1: A Brief History of the Internet.* New York: TV Books, L.L.C., 1999.

Vallee, Jacques F. *The Heart of the Internet: An Insider's View of the Origin and Promise of the On-Line Revolution.* Charlottesville, Va.: Hampton Roads Publishing Company, 2003.

White, Ron. *How Computers Work.* Indianapolis: Que Publishing/Pearson Education, 2008.

Winston, Brian. *Media Technology and Society: A History from the Telegraph to the Internet.* New York: Routledge, 1998.

Zahariadis, Anastasius, and Theodore Gavras. "The Future Internet: Future Internet Assembly 2011: Achievements and Technological Promises (Lecture Notes in Computer Science/

Computer Communication Networks and Telecommunications)."
New York: Springer, 2011.

Zittrain, Jonathan. *The Future of the Internet—And How to Stop It.*
Harrisonburg, Va.: R. R. Donnelley, 2009.

● ● ● FURTHER RESOURCES ● ● ●

BOOKS

Carr, Nicholas. *The Big Switch: Rewiring the World, from Edison to Google*. New York: W.W. Norton & Company, 2009.

Lambert, Laura, Chris Woodford, Christos J.P. Moschovitis, and Hilary Poole. *The Internet: A Historical Encyclopedia*. Santa Barbara, Calif.: ABC-CLIO, 2005.

Morgan, K., and J.M. Spector. *The Internet Society*. Billerica, Mass.: WIT Publishers, 2004.

DOCUMENTARIES AND DVDS

Internet Safety
The Safe Side LLC, 2006, DVD
Promotes online safety and features John Walsh, host of *America's Most Wanted* TV show.

Revolution OS
Wonderview Productions, 2001, DVD
A story about the Linux Operating System and the concept of "open source."

The History of Hacking
Discovery Channel, 2006
Interviews with leaders in the cybercrime field.

WEB SITES

Center for Democracy and Technology
http://www.cdt.org
The Center for Democracy and Technology works to keep the Internet open, innovative, and free.

The Center for Information Security Awareness
http://www.cfisa.org
This group works to increase security awareness among various community members.

The Children's Internet Protection Act (CIPA)
http://www.fcc.gov/guides/childrens-internet-protection-act
This federal law addresses offensive content viewable on school and library computers.

Computer Crime and Intellectual Property Section
http://www.cybercrime.gov
This section of the U.S. Department of Justice is responsible for implementing national strategies in combating computer and intellectual property crimes worldwide.

The Cyber Safety and Ethics Initiative
http://www.rrcsei.org/
A nonprofit group that provides research and professional development for teachers.

Department of Homeland Security
http://www.dhs.gov
This government agency is charged with protecting the United States from various threats.

Electronic Privacy Information Center
http://epic.org
EPIC focuses community members on privacy and civil liberties issues.

The Family Online Safety Institute
http://www.fosi.org
This Web site promotes best practices in the area of online safety with respect to free expression.

Federal Bureau of Investigation: Kids Page

http://www.fbi.gov/fun-games/kids/kids

The FBI provides information about investigation, safety, and other topics for kids.

Federal Communications Commission (FCC)

http://www.fcc.gov

The FCC regulates interstate and international communications.

Internet Crime Complaint Center

http://www.ic3.gov/default.aspx

Established by joint effort of the Department of Justice, Federal Bureau of Investigation, and the National White Collar Crime Center to document, research, and analyze complaints of Internet crime.

The Internet Keep Safe Coalition

http://www.ikeepsafe.org

This collaborative effort among government and public safety professionals works to disseminate safety resources to families worldwide.

Internet World Stats

http://www.internetworldstats.com

This site provides the latest statistics about the growth of the Internet

i-SAFE Inc.

http://www.isafe.org

This nonprofit group is dedicated to protecting to online activity experienced by youth.

The National Center for Missing and Exploited Children

http://www.missingkids.com

This organization serves as a national resource center for information and issues related to missing and exploited children.

National Cyber Security Alliance

http://staysafeonline.org

The NCSA provides support for digital citizens who use the Internet.

NetSmartz Workshop

http://www.netsmartz.org/parents

This Web site educates families and professionals about Internet concerns.

OnGuard Online

http://onguardonline.gov

OnGuard Online provides tips to assist you against computer crimes.

The Pew Research Center Internet and American Life Project

http://www.pewinternet.org

This think tank provides information on online safety and education.

United States Computer Emergency Readiness Team (US-CERT)

http://www.us-cert.gov

The United States Computer Emergency Readiness Team interacts with government entities, industry, and the community to defend against cyberattacks.

● ● ● INDEX ● ● ●

● ● ● ABOUT THE AUTHORS ● ● ●

DR. SAMUEL C. MCQUADE, III, currently serves as the professional studies graduate program director in the Center for Multidisciplinary Studies at the Rochester Institute of Technology (RIT). He holds a doctoral degree in public policy from George Mason University, and a master's degree in public administration from the University of Washington. He teaches and conducts research at RIT in areas inclusive of cybercrime, enterprise security, and career options in high-tech societies. Dr. McQuade has presented his research findings from this and other studies, along with its implications for Internet safety, information security, and cyberethics at major events hosted by: the American Society of Criminology, the British Society of Criminology, the U.S. Department of Homeland Security, the National Intelligence Council, the National Governors Association, the Berkman Center for Internet and Society at Harvard Law School, the Family Online Safety Institute, the Division on Addictions of Harvard Medical School, and the National Association of State Chief Information Officers. Previous books include *Understanding and Managing Cybercrime* (Pearson, 2006), *The Encyclopedia of Cybercrime* (Greenwood, 2009) and *Cyber Bullying: Protecting Kids and Adults from Online Bullies* (Praeger, 2009).

SARAH E. GENTRY is currently a graduate student in the professional studies master's of science degree program at the Rochester Institute of Technology with course concentrations in security technology management and business. She has worked as a system administrator for both the RIT residential computing lab and the Society for the Protection and Care of Children in Rochester, NY. Sarah holds a bachelor's of applied arts and science degree in multidisciplinary studies also from RIT.

ABOUT THE
● ● ● CONSULTING EDITOR ● ● ●

MARCUS K. ROGERS, PH.D., is the director of the Cyber Forensics Program in the department of computer and information technology at Purdue University, a former police officer, and the editor in chief of the *Journal of Digital Forensic Practice*. He has written, edited, and reviewed numerous articles and books on cybercrime. He is a professor, university faculty scholar, and research faculty member at the Center for Education and Research in Information Assurance and Security. He is also the international chair of the Law, Compliance and Investigation Domain of the Common Body of Knowledge (CBK) committee, chair of the Ethics Committee for the Digital and Multimedia Sciences section of the American Academy of Forensic Sciences, and chair of the Certification and Test Committee – Digital Forensics Certification Board. As a police officer he worked in the area of fraud and computer crime investigations. Dr. Rogers sits on the editorial board for several professional journals. He is also a member of various national and international committees focusing on digital forensic science and digital evidence. Dr. Rogers is the author of books, book chapters, and journal publications in the field of digital forensics and applied psychological analysis. His research interests include applied cyberforensics, psychological digital crime scene analysis, cybercrime scene analysis, and cyberterrorism. He is a frequent speaker at international and national information assurance and security conferences, and guest lectures throughout the world.